Modern Witchcraft Guide for Beginners

Starter Kit of Wiccan History & Traditions; Practical Magick, Spells & Rituals with Crystals, Candles, & Herbs for the Solitary Practitioner

Author:
Glinda Porter

TABLE OF CONTENTS

INTRODUCTION

Witch. What image does that word conjure up for you? The old Hollywood version of the hag with a mole on her nose, cackling as she flies across the backdrop of a full moon? Or perhaps the new Hollywood version of a pretentious English boarding school with mystical creatures hiding behind every door? I hate to be the bearer of bad news, but both images are equally incorrect.

The modern witch is your local baker, the CEO of a Fortune 500 company, that florist down the street, or the mail delivery person who waves at you every morning. The modern witch is physically indistinguishable from you and me (and very rarely has a lightning bolt scar on their forehead). The modern witch could be anyone who wants to unlock their highest potential, achieve their deepest desires, and delve into the powers held within themselves.

Getting started in witchcraft and/or the Wiccan religion can feel like a gargantuan task. Reliable information is scattered over many sources and can be difficult to differentiate from the misunderstood, incorrect, and just outright dangerous. But you can take a deep breath and relax. All the information, spells, rituals, etc. found in this book have been researched and comes from a practicing Wiccan witch. Everyone working on the spiritual plane was once a beginner picking their way through a mountain of information, spells, and theory. But what was once a long, arduous process brought with trial and error, has been distilled and explained simply within this book.

This book will give you a great head start in gaining the knowledge and unlocking the abilities you need to begin your own personal journey into the world of witchcraft and Wicca. We will be discussing everything you need to know to get up and going, including:

• A history of Wicca and Witchcraft

- Beliefs, practices, and common rituals
- The difference between Wicca and Witchcraft
- An introduction to Wicca
- The seasons, holidays, and celebrations of the Wiccan calendar
- Step-by-step instructions to help you with basic rituals
- Simple spells to get started
- The relationship to nature, and the Gods/Goddesses
- Working within the spirit world

Although it is important to have a background and understanding of the theory behind spell work, practical and doable instructions for spells is what can lead to actual changes in your life. With that in mind, I have included over **45 simple spells** to attract money, draw good luck and love into your life, and protect yourself from evil - these are everything you need as a new witchcraft or Wiccan practitioner (or as an experienced witch looking for a refresher or some new spells).

We will learn to tap into our own magic as you are guided through each step of these Wiccan and witchcraft practices, including details on personalizing them to your specific situation. You will gain confidence in your own knowledge, inner force, and intuition. Learning to discover and harness your natural talents to perform work in the spirit realm will open up an entirely new world of possibilities.

We will dive deep into the world of moon, candle, herb, crystal, and incense magic, bask in appreciation for the natural elements of the universe, and walk beside the various Gods and Goddesses which inhabit the spiritual plane.

One very important lesson to learn in the pursuit of knowledge and magick is who you can trust. There are plenty of charlatans out there looking to separate you from your money at any cost; people who have never cast a spell in their life, writing books and "advice blogs" with absolutely zero real-life experience in the art of witchcraft. It can be devastating and dangerous to perform spell work that you do not understand or that has not been properly vetted. So, with that being said, let me tell you about my introduction to Wicca and witchcraft - the good, the bad, and the ugly.

I was introduced to Wicca, and eventually witchcraft, in 1994 through a friend. Once he realized it wasn't some kind of instant, get rich quick thing, he lost interest. But a belief system that properly appreciated and praised the beauty of nature was exactly what I was looking for. So, I began researching and practicing as a solitary practitioner. By 1995, I was a wide-eyed, fledgling Wiccan. Not all Wiccans are witches, and not all witches are Wiccan. However, my intent was to practice spell work within the Wicca belief system. Being new to the belief system and living in a rural setting, I did not have experienced Wiccans around me to provide guidance. Google did not even exist and the internet as a whole was still in its infancy. What I did have was access to a bookstore. So, I began to read everything I could to learn the ins and outs of the religion, as well as spell casting. I collected over a hundred spell books, not to mention the books on Wicca theology, symbology, and divination.

One of the biggest problems that I faced in those early days was understanding how to wade through so many spells which promised the same result but required the use of such different materials, tools, and incantations. Despite all of my reading, I had never found a source that explained to me how the spiritual realm actually worked or the reasoning behind the actions taken within a spell or ritual. They were all very good at telling me *what* to do but fell very short in explaining *why* I was doing it. Learning through trial and error was dangerous and I made some huge mistakes, including saddling myself with a demonic attachment instead of the intended positivity and prosperity! I remember thinking how ridiculous it seemed that I could be surrounded by books specifically written for a beginning solitary practitioner, and yet none of them contained a compilation of all the things I truly **needed** to know. From those first few baby steps onto the astral plane, and the ensuing years of study and practicing, comes the book I wish had existed for me — this book.

To practice any type of religion or belief system, there are certain items that are either necessary or, at the very least, recommended, and Wicca or witchcraft are no different. But fear not, because we will be discussing how you can begin building your witchcraft toolkit through different types of altars, crystal balls, divination accessories, wands, and knives.

Whether you have never approached this amazing world of realms, inner power, nature and magick, or have been practicing for years, you are about to embark on a journey of discovery unlike any other. So, secure your third eye in the overhead compartment, strap in and let's take your life to a whole new level.

And may I be the first to greet you officially - "Merry Meet"!

CHAPTER 1 -
UNDERSTANDING AND
BENEFITS

Introduction to Witchcraft

There are an amazing amount of misconceptions about witchcraft; even as far as something seemingly as simple as providing a definition. The Merriam-Webster Dictionary definition of "witchcraft" is:

> "The use of sorcery or magic; communication with the devil or with a familiar; rituals and practices that incorporate belief in magic and that are associated especially with neo-pagan traditions and religions (such as Wicca)."

How can a single word have these three diametrically opposed definitions? Sorcery! Communication with the devil! A belief in magic associated with traditions and religions!

First and most importantly, modern witchcraft is NOT used to communicate with the devil! This is an example of how the folklore and superstitions of the past have bled into the present and continue to color the practice today.

In a general sense, witchcraft *should* be defined as behaviors that fall under the casting of spells that either have a positive or negative effect on the individual who is the focal point of the spell. Yes, witchcraft can be used to have negative effects on people; referred to as "black magick". However, we will be staying on the positive, affirming, "white magick" side of witchcraft. Witchcraft should be an act that promotes self-awareness, healing, and all-around the well-being of an individual.

The beautiful part of witchcraft is that it is completely driven by YOU! There is no liturgical or holy book, there are no services to attend every week, and there are no donation plates to pass around. Your witchcraft practice is dependent on your own intent on your time. The world is your sanctuary.

13

Brief History of Witchcraft

As much as I would love to be able to lay out an exacting history of witchcraft, with all of its twists and turns, I simply cannot. It would be very similar to writing down an exacting history of plants… all of them. Since modern humans began to cluster together and care for each other, there have been "witches". They may have been referred to as healers, shaman, soothsayers, sorcerers, or any number of other terms throughout the ages, but their title within a given point in history does not make them any less a "witch" by the modern standard.

The first written record of the term "witch" comes from the Bible. In the book of 1 Samuel, written between 931 B.C. and 721 B.C., King Saul is said to have sought the Witch of Endor in order to summon the spirit of a dead prophet. Apparently, in the days of King Saul, consorting with a witch was acceptable. But by the time of Exodus, the opinion of the "witch" had soured - Exodus 22:18 says, "thou shalt not suffer a witch to live." So, yes, the Bible hasn't exactly been a great book for us throughout time.

The superstitious and the ignorant blamed witches for pretty much every disease, natural disaster, societal ill and stubbed toe since the medieval period. The term "witch" became synonymous with a woman who worshipped the devil, made unholy agreements, used the powers of black magick to cause harm, and lured pure souls into darkness. Being accused of being a "witch" would get you executed, but being a "sorcerer" would get you a royal appointment. A "sorcerer" was seen as an individual who used magick in furtherance of the wishes of the king. Not surprisingly for the time period, women were considered "witches" and men were considered "sorcerers". What? You didn't think sexism was a modern invention, did you?

How witches and witchcraft was viewed in society has been dependent upon the culture and their religious beliefs. For instance, healers and shamans are/were venerated and respected members of the community in the African and South American cultures. However, as a general rule, the more Christianized that a culture became, the more witchcraft was pushed to the outskirts of acceptability. Contact with the spirit realm was seen as demonic or in the service of the devil. The Christian God and his Son, Jesus Christ, exist for believers on the spiritual plane. However, for them, God, Jesus Christ, and the Holy Spirit are the only entities allowed to perform work on the spiritual plane. Any other work is considered "blasphemy".

Perhaps nowhere better exemplifies the zealous behavior of Christianity run wild than Salem, Massachusetts in 1692-1693. The Salem Witch Trials. The ironic part about the Salem Witch Trials is that there may not have been even one actual witch. The truth of the matter is that Puritan beliefs led to the punishment and deaths of 25 people. Of those twenty-five individuals, nineteen were executed by hanging, five died while in jail awaiting trial, and one died from being crushed under rocks. The entire period of "trials" was really more of a kangaroo court with no chance of survivability. The accused would be strapped to a dunk board (picture a large teeter-totter positioned either on a low bridge or on the bank of a body of water). The accused would be strapped to the board and lowered into the water. The Puritans believed that water was a pure element and would not accept the unclean. Therefore, if the accused sank and drowned in the river, then they were posthumously declared innocent. If the accused floated back up and lived through the trial, she was found guilty of witchcraft and was executed. With 25 people who died as a result of being found guilty, it is unclear how many individuals died as a result of the test itself.

Any history of witchcraft would be incomplete without a history of modern Wicca. Wicca is the nature-based religion surrounding the act of witchcraft.

The "father" of modern Wicca is Gerald Gardner, although he never actually called his belief system "Wicca" because he preferred the more ancient term "Witchcraft". In 1920, Gardner was initiated into the New Forest Coven in Britain. It was Gardner's belief and claim that the

New Forest Coven was a surviving group of original witch-cult members.

In 1946, Gardner feared that witchcraft was a dying and disappearing practice. So he began his own coven, calling it the Bricket Wood Coven, with another former member of the New Forest Coven, Edith Woodford-Grimes. Gardner and Woodford-Grimes became the High Priest and High Priestess of the Bricket Wood Coven. Gardner implanted in his new tradition a lasting foundation of Wicca - the notion of an equal God and Goddess (this was terrifically unique and intriguing within the patriarchal, male-dominated society of 1940s Britain). In this same year, Gardner initiated Alex Sanders into the Bricket Wood Coven. Sanders would later leave Bricket Wood Coven to form a new system of belief known as Alexandrian Wicca.

Woodford-Grimes only stayed with the Bricket Wood Coven for 6 years, citing concerns over the publicity that Gardner was attempting to bring to the religion. Prior to Gardnerian Witchcraft, all aspects of witchcraft were practiced in extreme privacy for the safety of the practitioners. Gardner, however, aimed to change the pact of secrecy of the religion and to gain popular understanding and acceptance. This proved to be a brilliant and well-timed strategy, but it did tend to make some traditionalists rather uneasy.

In 1953, Gardner initiated Doreen Valiente into the Bricket Wood Coven and she became the new High Priestess of the coven. With the assistance of Valiant, Gardner wrote the Bricket Wood Coven Book of Shadows. Many of the rituals in the Book of Shadows came from late Victorian-era occultism, but much of the spiritual content is derived from older pagan religions and includes both Hindu and Buddhist influences. Valiant was able to rewrite many of the spells and incantations into poetic verse. The partnership with Valiant was also short-lived, as she left the coven due to Gardner's continued publicity hunt and the new rules and restrictions which he began placing on the Bricket Wood Coven and the other covens following Gardnerian Witchcraft.

Gardnerian Witchcraft was brought to the United States in the 1960s by a British Airways employee named Raymond Buckland and his wife. The Bucklands were initiated into Witchcraft in Britain by Monique Wilson, a Gardner adherent. Upon their move to the United States, the Bucklands began the Long Island Coven. The Bucklands continued to lead the Long Island Coven until 1973, at which time the Bucklands stopped strictly following Gardnerian Witchcraft and formed a new tradition called Saex Wicca. Saex Wicca combined aspects of Gardnerian Witchcraft with Anglo-Saxon pagan iconography.

In 1971, American Zsuzsanna Budapest fused Wiccan practices with the burgeoning feminist ideals and politics to form Dianic Wicca. This tradition focused exclusively on the Goddess, Diana, and was completely made of female practitioners.

Although there are many different offshoots of Wicca and types of witchcraft, as we will soon see, Gardnerian Witchcraft was the first to step out of the shadows and show itself as a legitimate religious belief.

Basic Principles, Beliefs, and Practices of Wicca

Wicca is the "religion" of witchcraft. As we have seen, there is no central dogma, no governing body, and no unifying holy book for Wicca. So, if you ask ten Wiccans their spiritual beliefs, you are likely to get ten different answers. However, there are some core principles and beliefs which are common to the vast majority of modern Wiccan sects. Let's explore some of these overarching beliefs.

Wicca acknowledges the **duality** of the divine, meaning that both the male and female aspects of divinity - a God and a Goddess. Depending upon the tradition that the Wiccan ascribes to, the God and Goddess can be known by many different names: Isis and Osiris, Cerridwen and Herne, Apollo and Athena, etc. There are even traditions that honor a non-gender specific deity (still encompassing both the male and female aspects, but not identified as "male" and "female"). In many Gardnerian sects, the names of the honored deities are revealed only to initiated members and kept secret from all people outside of their sect.

The concept of duality is an overarching theme of Wicca. For light to exist, there must be darkness; for good to exist, there must be evil; for a sun, there must be a moon; for life, there must also be death. It is within this duality that respect and an awe for nature are found. Nature is the perfect example for all duality - out of life comes death, out of death comes life. As the plant is eaten by the rabbit, the rabbit must die and surrender its nutrients back to the soil for a new plant to grow. Wiccans hold nature in the highest regard for its perfect balance of duality, exemplifying the God and Goddess. We mourn the death and at the same time celebrate the life to come.

Within covens, we find the traditions of **initiation** and the **system of degrees**. Initiation is a formal acceptance into witchcraft and into a coven. It is a symbolic rebirth into the faith wherein you dedicate yourself to the God and/or Goddess of the chosen tradition. An initiation is akin to baptism in the Christian faith. Although initiation is usually observed by those joining a coven, it is certainly possible to undergo initiation as a solitary practitioner. Within Wicca, there is not a specific title of practitioner who is responsible for taking the prayers of believers before the God and Goddess. We are all sacred beings and interaction with the God and Goddess is not limited just to the priesthood or a select group of individuals. Anyone with the proper intent can approach the deities. As such, the solitary practitioner can perform their own initiation.

The degree system is used solely within covens. Degrees are obtained through the dedication of time to the religion and through study. A first degree is obtained at the time of initiation, a second degree can be obtained following 6 months of being in the faith and studying the craft, and the third degree can be obtained after 1 year and 1 day of being in the faith and studying the craft. In order to be named a High Priest or High Priestess of a coven, you need to have obtained a third degree.

The belief in and use of **magick** is nearly a universal principle among Wiccans. Magick is viewed within Wicca as the redirection of natural forces through manipulation on the spirit plane in order to realize or manifest the intent of the practitioner. This is where evil can become a problem within Wicca. There are spells (curses) that can be used to cause injury or negativity to occur to another individual. In order to perform that type of magick (black magic), the intent of the practitioner must be evil. The intent of the practitioner is extremely important to spell work. Magick can be used for good or magick can be used for evil and, oftentimes, the difference is found in the heart (the intent) of the practitioner.

The importance of keeping to the white side of magick cannot be understated. A guiding principle within witchcraft is the **Rule of Three** found within the **Wiccan Rede**. The definition of "Rede" is: "Advice passed on to another." The Wiccan Rede states as follows:

> "Bide the Wiccan Law ye must,
> in perfect love and perfect trust.
> Eight words the Wiccan Rede fulfill;
> If ye harm none, do what ye will.
>
> What ye send forth comes back to thee,
> so ever mind the Rule of Three.
> Follow this with mind and heart,
> Merry ye meet and merry ye part."

The Rule of Three states that any dark magick one performs will be returned to the witch threefold. Fear and respect for the Rule of Three, along with morality, is what keeps the white witch from performing painful, destructive, and disturbing black magick spells or rituals.

Wiccans, regardless of their tradition, hold the principle of **personal responsibility** near and dear. Everyone is responsible for their own actions. Whether a member of a coven or a solitary practitioner, we must all be willing to accept the consequences, both good and bad, of our behavior here on the physical plane and in the spiritual plane.

And the final overarching principle of Wicca is **respect for the beliefs of others**. You will not see Wiccans out on a street corner professing why you also should become a Wiccan. Each person has the right and, indeed, the responsibility to choose their own spiritual path. Quite frankly, Wicca is not for everyone. If the beliefs and principles of Wicca do not fall in line with your personal beliefs, find a different path. It is important for the conviction of the Wiccan that they search out Wicca, not have Wicca thrust upon them, nor should they expect everyone around them to convert to Wicca. Although we do not necessarily receive the same from other organized religions, Wiccans are to fully respect the spiritual beliefs of others.

The Role of The Sun

Although witchcraft and Wicca generally bring to mind thoughts of spells and rituals cast by moonlight, the sun plays an equally important role. The sun is the realm of the God and is seen as the masculine aspect of the daily cycle. The God is often referred to and depicted as the Horned God, his horns thought to be a symbol of virility. The Horned God is also usually seen as having the upper half of a man and the bottom half of a goat, much like the vision of Pan in earlier Pagan religions.

Another form common to the God in modern Wicca is that of the Green Man. Within this iteration, the God's natural forest aspect is brought to the forefront. The God is connected with the sun, hunting, death, forests, and animals.

Any spells or rituals having to do with the more "masculine" powers of hunting, death, forestry, plant life, or animals would, as such, be performed with honorifics to the God in whatever form to which you ascribe. These spells and rituals would most effectively be performed during the day and while the sun is at its peak in the sky.

Sunlight can also be used to charge magickal items, or to imbue non-magickal items with magickal properties, to be used in the realm of the God. For instance, perhaps you are a bowhunter. On the day prior to your hunt, leave your bow and arrows in the sunlight. Allow these daily items to become more than mere tools of your own ability, but feel that they have been soaked in the God's power.

Or follow the tradition of the Vikings who would place their axes outside their dwellings on sun-filled days, but never allow moonlight to touch them as they believed moonlight would dull the blade by stealing its virility. As an aside, it is this tradition that led, through the twists of many generations, to the practice of a fighter or soldier not engaging in sexual encounters in the days leading up to a fight, lest he "lose his edge".

Also, due to the elliptical orbit of Earth, the sun is not always the same distance from us. The Earth is at its closest to the sun in the first week of January, known as "perihelion", and at its farthest from the sun in the first week of July, known as "aphelion". So from January to July, the bond between the Earth and the sun (the bond between us and the God) is weakened by each day; and from July to January, that bond grows stronger each day. Wiccans and witches use our position relative to other celestial bodies to time spells, rituals, and holidays for the greatest effect.

The Role of The Moon

No other object holds as much symbolism to Wicca as the moon. The moon is the realm of the Goddess, the feminine aspect of the daily cycle. In line with the duality of Wicca, the Goddess is the antithesis of the God in all things. So, in relief of the hunter, killer, animalistic God, comes the rejuvenating, life-giving, magickal, human-loving Goddess.

As we have discussed earlier, the Goddess can be known by a wide pantheon of names. The most common in modern Wicca, however, is "Diana" of the Greek tradition. I have always found it telling that the masculine, hunting, "tough guy" aspect of the duality would be known as the Green Man (which seems mysterious and kept at arm's length), while the feminine, nurturing, motherly aspect would be known as Diana (a more relatable, human, and welcoming name).

Traditionally in Wicca, the Goddess is seen as a "Triple Goddess", meaning that she embodies the aspects of maiden, mother, and crone. She is at once the eternal virgin as well as the bringer of life. The Triple Goddess symbol has, in more recent times, been adopted as a universal symbol for Wicca and witchcraft. The symbol is the three moon phases connected at tangents – the waxing crescent moon, the full moon, and the waning crescent moon.

Moonlight is the raining down of the Goddess' love and life forces onto her adherents. Because of this deep connection, moonlight is used in a large number of spells, rituals, and celebrations. Moonlight is also used to charge any crystal or magickal item with positive energy.

The moon's phases also play a large part in the effectiveness of spell work, not in that it is necessary to only cast spells or perform rituals on full moons. In fact, the waxing (building up) and waning (breaking down) phases can also be key depending on what type of spell or ritual is being performed. Also, the new moon phase (rejuvenating of power) is suggested for many spells because of its universal openness and promise of things to come.

Most spells found in books or online will have suggested moon phases in which they should be performed. However, if they do not, match the spell's intention with the proper moon phase - A new moon is best for spells to manifest new joys, emotions, or powers into your life; a waxing moon is best for spells that increase existing joys, emotions, or powers; a full moon is best for maintenance spells, devotional spells, or spells of protection from evil; and a waning moon is best for spells which decrease bad habits or negative emotions in our lives.

Sabbats

The 8 major "holidays" of Wicca are referred to as "Sabbats". The exact timing of each Sabbat is based upon the solstices and equinoxes, as well as the moon phase. The yearly Sabbats equally divide the calendar and are often represented by a circle divided into 8 sections (picture an empty Trivial Pursuit game piece). This circle is called the Wheel of The Year.

- Yule - Midwinter Solstice. Usually occurring in December. Common practices are giving of gifts, feasting, decorating using sprigs of holly, mistletoe, ivy, yew, and pine (known as the "Yule Log"), bringing in and decorating of an evergreen tree.

- Imbolc - Candlemas. Imbolc falls on February 1st. It marks the earliest rumblings of the forthcoming spring (in the northern hemisphere). It is commonly used as a time for

32

pledges, rededication, initiations, purification, and cleaning.

- Ostara - Ostara marks the vernal equinox. It is a time when the day and the night are equal and balanced. Ostara is celebrated as a time of new beginnings and of life emerging from the deadly grip of winter.

- Beltane - Known as "May Day" in the modern world. As in ancient Irish pagan religions, the day is celebrated by dancing around the maypole. The festival of Beltane is meant to recognize life at its fullest, the greening of the world, and youth.

- Litha - Summer Solstice. Litha falls at the end of June/early July. It marks the day when the sun shines the longest during the year. Litha is a highly anticipated celebration each year and festivities have been known to last 24-36 hours.

- Lammas - Also known as Lughnasadh. This is the only festival dedicated to specifically honoring and celebrating the God. It is traditionally celebrated by baking and eating bread in the figure of the God. Lammas is meant to symbolize the sanctity and importance of the upcoming harvest. This is the first of three harvest festivals.

- Mabon - Autumnal Equinox. Mabon typically falls in September. Mabon is a celebration of thanksgiving for the fruits of the earth and a recognition of the need to share the bounty to secure blessings during the harsh upcoming winter months. It is the second of the three harvest festivals.

- Samhain - Halloween. The third harvest festival. Samhain (pronounced sow-wen) is a night-long celebration of the lives of the dead; paying respects to passed relatives, elders of faith, and loved ones. In some rituals, the dead are invited to attend the festivities along with the living. It is considered a night festival during which the veil between the world of the living and the world of the dead is at its thinnest allowing for movement between worlds and easier communication across the plains.

Being a Wiccan and Being a Witch

Being Wiccan does not necessarily mean you are a witch, and being a witch does not necessarily mean you are Wiccan. However, practicing modern Wicca *nearly always* involves practicing witchcraft. It is for this reason that I believe we can comfortably call all Wiccan followers "witches", but we cannot assume that all witchcraft practitioners are "Wiccan".

Wicca is a religious belief. Witchcraft is an action. Think of it this way, Christianity is a religious belief, while prayer is an action. All Christians pray, but not everyone who prays is a Christian.

What separates a Wiccan who practices witchcraft from a practitioner of witchcraft is the belief in the Wiccan Rede/Rule of Three. A Wiccan believes that any negativity or any evil released onto the spiritual plane, intentionally doing harm to another, will be returned to the caster threefold. A witchcraft practitioner believes that there is no consequence to them personally regardless of the energy released during the casting of a spell.

Magick and how it Can Help You

Have you thought the use of the "k" at the end of magick was a typo? It is not. Magick with a "k" is the spelling of the word which differentiates what witches practice versus magic with a "c" which is the sleight of hand which magicians and illusionists perform. Magic with a "c" pulls a rabbit out of a hat, while magick with a "k" casts a spell to free a rabbit from being held captive in a hat.

Now, how can magick help you? Magick is an action meant to materialize a blessing, something that the spell caster has set their intentions upon. Magick is a result of intent. The intent of the castor of a spell

36

functions differently on the spiritual plane than it does here on the physical plane. Magick (through manifestation) can provide changes in our lives through manipulation of energies and vibrational frequencies.

I am often asked, "If you are a witch, why not just do a spell to win the lottery or materialize a new car." Trust me, those questions will come your way sooner than you think. My response is usually along the lines of "It just doesn't work that way." You will find spell books that include spells for material possessions (money, a new house, a new car, etc.). However, that does not mean that, if you perform this spell you will awaken tomorrow morning and trip over stacks of $100 bills. You must remember that we work on a spiritual plane, an ethereal dimension, where energy is the only material and time is irrelevant. A spell to manifest money may present itself in your life as a more lucrative job opportunity, or a gift from someone, or an inheritance, etc. Magick can and will help you manifest your desires in your life, but most times we do not have the ability to dictate just *how* those desires arrive. This is the very factor that makes magick so useful in other areas.

Magick seems ready-made for self-improvement pursuits, such as introspection, control of negative emotion, enhancement of positive emotion, finding love, spiritual growth and enlightenment, protection from negative and evil forces, healing both physically and emotionally, discovering and developing psychic abilities, etc. These are the types of areas wherein magick reveals its true capabilities and its nature. Yes, materialism is certainly a part of the world and a part of each Wiccan as well, however, it should not be the main focus or the impetus which draws the practitioner. One must always remember that in Wiccan belief, there is a balance in all things. Therefore, there is a negative to every positive and the adherent must be willing to accept that negative as readily as the positive.

Different Types of Witchcraft and Magick

There is a seemingly endless number of types of witchcraft and magick which one can practice. It seems that there are as many categories, sub-categories, and specializations as there are practitioners! But let's focus on 7 categories.

Folk Magick - A "traditional" or "Folk Witch" practices the magick of his or her ancestors, or of their general geographic region. The Folk Witch tends to take their magick as historical because it would have been practiced well prior to the formation of Wicca as a religion. The Folk Witch would most likely be a wealth of local information, having access to local availability of talismans, crystals, herbs, charms, and spells. Many Folk Witches have begun to blend the use of their "traditional" magick with more updated beliefs and modern tools.

Green Magick - The Green Witch focuses on their interaction with nature and the magic to be garnered daily from nature itself. A Green

Witch is typically a rural witch and highly influenced by folk magic, with the center of their magical world being the home. The use of herbal remedies tends to be the specialty of most Green Witches and they often grow and harvest the herbs themselves, as opposed to purchasing herbs from vendors. Also, Green Witches are usually quite versed in aromatherapy using local herb blends.

Gardnerian Wiccans - Gardnerian Wiccans are one of only two forms of modern witchcraft that can trace its lineage back in an unbroken line to the very beginning of Wicca, i.e., Gerald Gardner. Gardnerian Wicca is a British form of Wicca which is bound by oath to practice reasonable witchcraft. Gardnerian Wicca tends to be extremely practical with very little ceremony.

Alexandrian Wiccans - Alexandrian Wiccans are the second form of modern witchcraft able to trace its lineage back to those early days, i.e., Alex Sanders. Alex Sanders was one of Gerald Gardner's very first initiates into Wicca. Alexandrian

Wicca is typically a blend of ceremonial and Gardnerian Wicca.

Eclectic Witchcraft - Eclectic witchcraft is a catch-all term for witchcraft that doesn't specifically fit into any other category. The Eclectic Witch may be a blend of many different traditions, faiths and folk practices. The Eclectic Witch can be thought of as the consummate do-it-yourselfer. They may take some traditional beliefs, some things read online, some things learned from a workshop they attended, and their own personal experiences; roll them all together, and come up with a practical method of witchcraft that works for them.

Ceremonial Magick - Ceremonial witchcraft, also called High witchcraft, uses very specific tools and incantations to call upon the deities and entities of the spirit world. Ceremonial witchcraft is a blend of ancient occult/pagan teachings. This type of witchcraft is held highly secret and many practitioners do not even identify with the word "witch" at all out of an abundance of caution.

Hereditary Witchcraft - Hereditary witchcraft is a belief and practice system in which the knowledge is handed down from one generation to the next (mother to daughter; father to son). It is very unusual for any family outsider to be included in Hereditary witchcraft and it is just as unusual for the existence of such knowledge to even be discussed in the presence of an outsider, including sons-in-law or daughters-in-law. The relationship need not necessarily be a genetic one, as adopted children are seen as worthy candidates for Hereditary witchcraft. It is more a family tradition basis than a strictly biological tradition.

The Do's and Don'ts of Witchcraft

Starting to practice witchcraft or learning about the Wiccan belief system is hard, there is simply a TON of information and it feels like you need to instantly retain it all. Right? Relax. You are not going to go from "interested" in witchcraft to some full-blown, mega-wizard, master of all realities by reading a book one time. This is a huge opportunity to affect both your inner being and your physical life, but it is a process. For those times when you become overwhelmed at the length and breadth of the information available to you, and you will, I have compiled here a list of Witchcraft Do's and Don'ts so you can easily reference them later. Think of this as a cheat sheet of highlights for your magickal journey.

DO your homework. Research everything... twice! I say this for two reasons. First, if you are just starting out, you still need to determine if Wicca and/or witchcraft is really what you are looking for in your life. Take the time to research as many world religions as you can, compare and contrast your personal beliefs and feelings with the teachings and precepts of these religions, and then decide. Please understand, of course I want as many strong Wiccan brothers and sisters as possible and I want you all to experience the freedom that comes from practicing witchcraft to experience a more fulfilling life. But more than that, I hope that everyone finds their own personal path to happiness and peace. If that is through Wicca and/or witchcraft, welcome! If it is not, then go in peace and I wish you only joy on your journey.

DON'T rush out and spend a bunch of money on your ritual tools right away. The practice of witchcraft was being performed in times where purchasing items was not even a consideration. Everything necessary was made by hand. Now, thankfully for us craft-challenged individuals, we are able to buy some of the ritual items. That is nice but can get extremely expensive very quickly. So, until you are certain that you want to practice witchcraft or enter the Wiccan religion, and have researched what you will need to purchase versus what you can make for yourself, there is no need to run up that credit card bill.

DO choose your ritual items carefully and mindfully. Once you have made the commitment and decision to move forward into the Wiccan religion or practice of witchcraft, you will need a few items (a starter tool kit, if you will). Some things you may be able to make yourself. Others you may need to purchase. Take your time in finding these items. Hold them, touch them, feel their energy, and note the way your energy responds. This is not the time for bargain online shopping I'm afraid. Allow your intuition to guide you to the proper items through physical contact.

DON'T choose witchcraft out of a thirst for revenge. I am talking about hexes and curses here. Don't do it. That is the path of black magick. Yes, it exists. And no, it is in no way good for you. The type of negative energy that it takes to hex or curse a person marks you, that kind of evil stains you. Witchcraft and Wicca were not intended to be used to harm others. The side of light will lead to peace and balance - while darkness will always lead to destruction and decay.

DO commit to following the Rule of Three and the Wiccan Rede. It is human to be upset and out of a fit of anger wish some type of harm on another. But as a practitioner of witchcraft or Wicca, we need to end those negative thoughts quickly, before they turn to intent or action. By committing ourselves to the Wiccan Rede, the basic principle of which is "Do No Harm", we are committing ourselves to a world of light. Let that anger pass through you and move on. It is not worth the threefold return just to gain some fleeting moral victory. Let it go.

DON'T expect everything to turn out perfectly   instantaneously. Witchcraft is more an art than it is a science. Some spells just do not work for me. It happens. We may try the exact same spell using the exact same ingredients yet receive completely different results. It is no different than if you gave two artists the exact same type of brush, paint, and canvas, along with instruction to produce a painting of the same mythological animal. There is very little chance that their paintings would be identical. Do not let spell work that does not produce your desired result overly frustrate you. Keep a good, up-to-date grimoire so that you are able to see what works for you and what does not.

DO what feels best and works for you. Witchcraft is not a list of boxes to check off on the way to a promised prize. Witchcraft is the ultimate customizable life-changer. There is no *wrong* way to practice! As long as your intention is clear to you and you are staying on the white witch side of things, you do you. The spell calls for a copper bowl, but all you have at the ready is a Tupperware container? As long as you believe it will suffice, it will suffice. Halfway through a ritual and forget the exact language you are to recite? As long as what you say holds the same meaning and power to you, wing it. The spell calls for the use of thyme, but you are allergic to thyme? Rosemary it is. Remember that witchcraft is about your intent being manifested on this plane through the manipulation of forces and energies on the spiritual plane. Your intent is the key.

DON'T reject meditation. Meditation provides clarity through a knowledge of self. Knowledge of yourself strengthens your ability to remain grounded. Remaining grounded allows your focus to be on your intent. And your intent is what is released onto the spiritual plane, or into the universe, during a spell or ritual. You don't need to become some kind of monk, just give yourself 10 minutes per day, three or four times per week, to meditate. You will be surprised at the results it will have on your practice and the effectiveness of your spell work.

DO trust yourself while walking along this path. You have made the decision to participate in something which exists solely to create joy, peace, comfort, and happiness in your life and in the lives of those you care about. There are so many self-destructive ways you could be spending your time, ways that would only serve to hurt you and those you love in the long run. But instead, you have consciously chosen to embark on a journey to better your life. By learning and practicing spell work, rituals, and enhancing your natural psychic abilities, you are doing just that - walking toward a better and more fulfilling life.

Psychic Abilities and Divination

Psychic Abilities

Psychic abilities are not necessarily a precursor or a result of witchcraft or Wicca. However, the development of these abilities does seem to be extremely common in both the religion of Wicca and in the practice of witchcraft, and for good reason. Wicca and witchcraft require one to be very self-aware; a state achieved through deep introspection. The more comfortable that we are able to become with the true nature of ourselves through introspection, the more obvious and pronounced your natural psychic abilities become. That is why, if you spend 10 minutes at any Wicca or witchcraft event, you will get 15 offers to have a tarot reading performed for you.

Everyone has at least a small amount of natural psychic ability lying dormant within them. The question becomes whether or not they will discover, nurture, and grow this talent. There are different types of psychic abilities and a number of ways to explore and develop these abilities.

First, let's discuss the types of abilities:

- **Precognition** is the ability to know future events. A Precog may receive clear, definite messages or visions of the future, or they may receive more vague messages or even flashes of images and emotions.

- **Intuition**, or **intuitiveness**, is the ability to just "know" things. An Intuitive usually makes an excellent Tarot Card reader because they are able to interpret the meaning of the cards correctly for the client without knowing any specifics of the client's life.

- **Clairvoyance** is the ability to visualize situations or objects not within the physical space. A Clairvoyant is excellent at remote viewing and are the type of "psychics" used by police in locating missing people.

- **Empathy** is the ability to sense the feelings, emotions, and energies of other people. Empaths often find themselves to be very effective spiritual healers as they are able to sense disturbances in the energy fields of their clients, which lead them to a specific part of the body that may be causing a health issue. Empaths are also the most likely to be affected by negative energies given off by evil or negative spirits and, as such, often find themselves feeling drained or exhausted just by being in the presence of specific people.

- **Mediums** are individuals who are able to communicate with the spirit world through the use of spirit guides. Mediums may see and/or hear the spirits themselves and be able to hold a dialogue, or they may only receive messages via dreams or visions without the ability to control the messages, like a telephone call where you can hear the other person but they cannot hear you.

- **Telepathy** is the ability to communicate with another living individual by mental means alone. Telepaths have been referred to as "mind readers", but that is not completely accurate. In truth, a Telepath is able to receive messages from another individual AND send messages to another individual. The other individual need not be a developed Telepath themselves but does need to be focused on sending or receiving a message.

- **Telekinesis** is the ability to move a physical object using only the power of their mind (intent). A Telekinetic is the Jedi of the psychic world. Telekinesis is a rare ability and is a favorite of charlatans to fake.

As I stated earlier, everyone has at least a little psychic ability and talent tucked away within them. This ability can be drawn out through introspection and meditation. But what then? There are a number of ways that you can begin to develop your natural psychic ability further. Let's take a look at some of them.

- **Listen Intently to What Is Said AND What Is Not Said**

- When people have a conversation, there is as much to be gleaned and learned by what is omitted as there is in what is actually discussed. For example, let's say that you are having a passing conversation with a female friend. You say, "How are you doing?" And she answers, "I'm fine. The kids are doing good and growing like weeds." Although that seems like a positive answer, you will notice that she glanced over herself quickly and never even mentioned her husband. Perhaps they are not doing so well as a couple as she would have you believe. Learn to stretch your intuitive legs.

- **Deliberate Clarity**
  - Achieving deliberate clarity simply means becoming aware of everything around you. It is being purposefully observant - another word for this is "mindfulness". Pay attention to changes in the sunlight and shadows, notice a shift in the wind, note who enters a room and who exits. Take mental notes of everything.   Becoming

deliberately clear will help you by being able to separate real psychic messages from imagination and wishful thinking.

- **Meditation**
  - One of the best ways to develop intuition is to implement a regular schedule of meditation. When we meditate, we explore and open the depths of our subconscious mind. Intuitiveness is a function of the subconscious. Learn your way around so you are able to connect to your subconscious and retrieve those intuitive thoughts.

- **Trust Your Gut**
  - Your "gut feeling" is your intuition trying to express itself. Those feelings are your subconscious thoughts struggling to come to the surface. Pay attention. Explore those thoughts. Learn to trust your intuition and see where it takes you.

- **Journal**
  - Have you ever had a dream about a specific person or an event? Have you ever felt like something important was about to happen but didn't know exactly what? Write it down! Keep a journal so you can track your sensory messages and be able to review them for significance. It will help you gain confidence in your abilities and learn to trust them more. Of course, there will inevitably be messages you are never able to confirm. And that is okay. It doesn't mean that they were not accurate, it only means that you were not able to verify the message.

- **Practice Makes Perfect**
  - Well, practice may not make you "perfect", but it will make you better. Try learning about different forms of divination and, when you find one that interests you, keep practicing it until you can verify that the messages you are receiving are valid. When you have practiced enough, keep practicing! There is no finish line here, you can

always improve or learn new skills. Challenge yourself to stretch and grow by developing new skills and strengthening those you have begun to develop.

- **Test Yourself**
  - If you believe you are receiving messages from someone or someplace else, try to confirm it. When your phone rings, try to feel who is calling before checking the caller ID. When you are meeting a friend for coffee, focus and try to feel what kind of music they are listening to on the drive. Then ask them when they arrive. Simple exercises like this will help you develop your natural abilities. Never shy away from a chance to test yourself. And realize that, as you start out, you may well be wrong more often than you are right. But, hopefully, with practice, your correct percentage will rise to heights that will surprise you.

Divination

Divination is the practice of seeking knowledge of the future or the unknown through supernatural or magickal means. As with psychic abilities, there are many ways to practice divination and some may match better with your innate abilities than others. Let's discuss some of the practices and see if anything particularly resonates with you. If not, try them all until you find one that works best with your personal abilities.

- **Tarot Cards**
  - If you are not familiar with divination, it may seem as though someone who reads Tarot Cards is "predicting the future" through the cards. That is not exactly accurate. The cards provide an outline or a course of energy. It is the job of the reader to interpret the meanings and possible outcomes of the flow of energies.

- **Celtic Ogham**
  - The Ogham are mostly used as a divination tool by Wiccans who follow a Celtic tradition. In

this practice, the Ogham alphabet is inscribed on wooden dowels. The dowels are then dropped, and the message is interpreted by the reader.

- **Norse Rune Stones**
  - According to Norse pagan tradition, Odin created a set of sacred symbols, known as Runes, as a gift to humans. Over the ensuing centuries, the Runes evolved into a collection of 16 letters. Each of these Runic letters holds both a metaphorical and divinatory meaning. The reader casts the lot of 16 stones and interprets the message based on how each Rune is positioned and oriented.

- **Tea Leaves**
  - The reading of tea leaves became popular in the western world in the 17th century, although the Chinese have been using the method for divination for much, much longer. In this practice, a cup of unstrained tea is made and consumed by the reader. When the tea is gone and the leaves remain, the cup is swirled three times to distribute the leaves

into a pattern. The reader is then able to interpret the message based upon the pattern formed by the tea leaves. Today, there are even specially designed teacups with patterns and symbols inscribed onto the rim and sides of the cup to make the process of interpretation easier.

- **Pendulum**
  - Pendulum divination is one of the simplest forms to understand and interpret. This form is based on the asking of yes or no questions. Based upon the resulting pattern of a swing of the pendulum (usually a crystal at the end of a length of rope or chain), the yes or no answer is determined. The trick to this type of divination is not so much in interpreting the result as it is in learning to ask the right questions.

- **Osteomancy**
  - If you knew that "Osteomancy" meant "divination through reading bones", you were a step ahead of me! However, reading bones has been performed by

cultures all around the world for thousands of years. Although there are many techniques, the purpose is the same – foretelling the path of future energies through interpreting a cast of bones.

- **Scrying**
  - This practice of scrying can be done using a number of different types of medium – water, mirror, crystal ball, etc. Pretty much any reflective surface can be used for scrying, although you may have noticed a pattern in the three media I listed (water, mirror, and crystals are all energy enhancers). Scrying is practiced by entering a state, not unlike meditation wherein you access your subconscious mind while keeping the client's question at the forefront of the conscious mind. By directing your energy and brain waves into the chosen media, an image or message can become clear to the reader (usually visually), either physically visible within the media or as a subconscious vision. It is then the job of the reader to interpret the

message for the client. The practice of scrying does come with a caveat. When opening ourselves up to the spirit world in this manner and essentially becoming a blank slate for another realm to draw on, there is no guarantee that the entity answering your call is a being of light. In other words, much like with the use of Ouija Boards, once the doorway is opened, there is no way of knowing exactly what is going to step through. This puts the reader in spiritual, mental, and possibly physical danger during and after each reading. Explore, but be safe.

- **Numerology**
  - Many pagan spiritual traditions, as well as Wiccans and witchcraft practitioners, incorporate the practice of numerology. Numbers have great significance within the spiritual and magickal realms. Some numbers hold more power than others, and specific combinations of numbers can even be developed for magickal use in spell work. There are also links to be drawn between numbers and

planets and/or other celestial bodies.

- **Automatic Writing**
  - One of the most popular modern methods of divination is automatic writing. In this practice, the practitioner holds a writing instrument, enters into a meditation-like state, and allows words and messages to flow through them onto the paper without any conscious thought or effort. The idea of automatic writing is to channel the message from the spirit realm directly onto the paper without running the information through the practitioner's conscious mind first. I have personally even seen automatic writing practiced with the eyes closed, writing phrases, keywords, and drawing shapes or pictures. Following the writing, the practitioner usually offers to go through the writing with the client to attempt to "divine" meaning from what may seem like an incoherent jumble of words.

In the section on scrying, you will notice that I mentioned Ouija Boards. I would be remiss if I did not at least mention that Ouija Boards (otherwise known as "Talking Boards" or "Spirit Boards") are used as a tool of divination. I did not include Spirit Boards in the list because I feel that they are extremely unsafe. Yes, I have heard it before, "you are warning me about a board game made by Milton-Bradley". And I completely understand the ridicule of my hesitancy. However, allow me to explain why Spirit Boards are so dangerous.

The cardboard and plastic used to make a Spirit Board and planchet are not the issue. The problem is that the board itself only serves as a focal point. The true power of a Spirit Board comes from the player(s). Most of the time, a player goes into a Spirit Board session completely unprotected and having no idea the danger that they are placing themselves in. Imagine going from playing flag football to playing against an NFL team - oh and you do not have any pads or a helmet. That is essentially what is going on when the common person, or even an inexperienced witch, communicates using a Spirit Board.

When a Spirit Board session begins, the player(s) opens him/herself to the spiritual plane and hopes to come into contact with a positive entity. That is like throwing open the door of a shark cage and hoping that Nemo is who swims in with you. Sure, it may be a positive entity, but are you truly prepared to deal with the consequences if it is not? Are you actually willing to roll the dice that it is Nemo as opposed to a great white shark? Quite honestly, the risk is simply too high and unnecessary.

There is absolutely no way to determine what type of entity or energy is speaking to you through a Spirit Board. And once that door is opened and something has been invited onto our plane, it is not a simple task to return it. Evil exists. Evil is real. Evil will do what evil does - cause nothing but pain, chaos, and turmoil. So, while you may think you are speaking with your dearly departed Aunt Edna, truthfully you may have just become the next target of a fresh new demon.

For these reasons, I could not in good conscience include Spirit

Boards on the above list. I recommend that this type of divination be avoided for the safety of everyone involved.

CHAPTER 2 - PREPARING

Grounding and Drawing Energy

Do you realize what is happening at this very moment as you read or listen to these words? Your brain is experiencing a literal lightning storm. Billions of times per second, the neurons in your brain are firing electrical pulses of ions across tiny gaps (much like a spark plug), within the trail of each lightning bolt are charged particles of chemicals that relay a biological message to the accepting neuron, directing what it does next. And this process is repeated constantly throughout the brain, simultaneously. Our bodies, our brains, our thoughts, feelings, and emotions are all electrical impulses - they are energy. My body, your body, a slug, a cow, a fox, and a meerkat, every living organism in the physical world is made of energy. And where do we receive our charge? What is the power plant that can keep all of these electro-chemical machines running at full capacity? Mother Earth! Our planet generates a constant, radiating stream of electromagnetic energy. Within this natural link between us and our planet can be found all the energy that we will ever need throughout our lives, both physically and metaphysically speaking. It is like all living creatures are plugged into the same electrical outlet.

This relates to our discussion of magick in two ways. First, magick requires a large output of energy from the Wiccan or witch. It is, after all, a blast of our intentions sent out into the universe and across the spiritual plane. And secondly, we humans have a tendency to step on our own power cord and we end up getting "unplugged", unfulfilled, and unsure how to fix our problems.

There are two important steps that we must take to ensure our magick and our spell work are being done with the proper energy - creating an energy circuit by grounding ourselves and centering our energy.

Creating an Energy Circuit Through Grounding

For centuries, humans never had to worry about whether their energies were or were not properly grounded because they were very rarely out of direct contact with the earth. But today we wear rubber-soled shoes, live and work many stories above the planet, spend our time on asphalt, and drive in rubber-tired vehicles. When was the last time you were in direct contact with the surface of the earth? For many, it might have been years! After all, rubber, asphalt, wood, and plastic are all non-conductive, which means we all pretty much exist in a bubble separating ourselves from the natural energy flowing from the Earth. Now, please do not misunderstand. I am not trying to convince you to go full hermit, move to the forest, and walk around barefoot in the middle of nowhere. I am quite happy to have my modern conveniences. But that makes it all the more important to make a designated effort to ground our energy from time to time in order to recharge ourselves and to rid ourselves of negativity. We cannot make a working energy circuit with only a "positive" wire or with only a "negative wire". Just like the electricity flow in our homes, we need to have a full, uninterrupted circuit with a positive, negative, and ground wire.

If you happen to live in a rural setting with warm average temperatures year-round, then you have hit the grounding jackpot. Take off your shoes and take a walk through the forest. Be mindful of the connection you are making with the earth, take time to appreciate the feeling of being in your rightful place in the natural scheme and in your biome. Stand with the grass between your toes and visualize the positive energy of the earth flowing up through your left leg, all the way up to the top of your head, and down your right side back into the ground. As this positive energy enters you, it shoves any and all negativity that you have taken on out of the way ahead of it and out through the bottom of your right foot. Once you have only the positive, white light flowing in and out of you and all of the negative, dark energy has been removed and cleansed from you, picture the light growing and branching into every part of you, every cell of your body, until you simply appear to yourself to be made of the light energy. That is how you want to feel when approaching spell work or rituals or any other spirit plane tasks - like you are so full of energy that you ARE the energy.

If you do not live in a countryside utopia, or like me, you only have "no shoe" weather for about 3 months per year, it doesn't mean that you cannot ground yourself. First of all, find a park and when it is warm enough, take off your shoes. But any other time that you need to ground, you can accomplish it through intense visualization.

First, find a chair with a straight enough back that you can sit comfortably with both of your feet flat on the floor. Close your eyes. Take 3 deep breaths, slowly in and slowly out. With each exhale, visualize roots extending from the bottom of your feet and going straight down towards the ground. By the third exhale, these roots reach all the way from wherever you are sitting, through the structure you are in, and into the ground beneath. Next, visualize the positive energy of the earth flowing up through your left leg, all the way up to the top of your head, and down your right side back into the ground. As this positive energy enters you, it shoves any and all negativity that you have taken on out of the way ahead of it and out through the bottom of your right foot. Once you have only the positive, white light flowing in and out of you and all of the negative, dark energy has been removed and cleansed from you, picture the light growing and branching into every part of you, every cell of your body, until you simply appear to yourself to be made of the light energy. That is how you want to feel when approaching spell work or rituals or any other spirit plane tasks - like you are so full of energy that you ARE the energy.

Centering Your Energy

Learning to center your energy is one of those big breakthrough moments in life. Being centered is a necessity in spell work, but it is also useful in daily, mundane life as well. It is all about controlling our emotional responses to stress and channeling them into a positive outcome.

Let's think about it this way. Have you ever had to give a speech or presentation in front of a group of people? You know that feeling of "butterflies" you had beforehand, the sweaty palms, the dry mouth, the increased heart rate, how it seemed like time was actually speeding up? That was your body responding to the stress you were under by dumping adrenaline into your bloodstream. Then came all of those negative thoughts about not being properly prepared, not being as eloquent as you should be, tripping over your words, and coming off as awkward instead of relaxed. Well, what if I told you that at that moment, just before you were ready to stand up and start speaking, you could visualize your way to using all of that adrenaline to your advantage? It is very similar when we are working on the spiritual plane, casting a spell, or performing a ritual. We get nervous that we are not prepared or are going to forget something. So, let's see how to center our energy and use all of that adrenaline to our advantage.

First, concentrate on your breathing. Take slow, deep breaths in through the nose and out through the mouth. This will flood your cells with oxygen as well as work to slow your heart rate to a reasonable level.

Secondly, know or figure out where your center is. This is your physical center of gravity. Usually, it is located about two fingers below your navel. This is the spot on your body with the greatest ability to balance. Focus on your center.

Next, visualize all of the energy in your body as being spread out into the points furthest from your center. For most, this will be your hands, feet and, top of your head. Visualize yourself pulling all of this scattered energy into your center. This energy becomes a super dense, bright light at your center.

Then visualize everything that is left in the places where your energy had been as a dark "Silly Putty" substance. Picture pulling all of this negativity, all of the negative thoughts, the worries, the stress of the situation out into the palms of your hands and shaping it into a ball. Then throw all of those lies and self-deprecation as far from you as you possibly can.

Now as you relax, you will feel a renewed sense of calm and confidence. You are once again clean and full of light. You are able to see your intentions clearly and are able to channel your adrenaline into positive thoughts.

You are centered.

Getting Clear with Your Intentions

It can be so disheartening to spend time and energy learning, preparing, and casting a spell just to have it not produce any results. You could have found the perfect spell and performed everything flawlessly, but nothing happens. I learned long ago that in times like these, it is usually a problem with intention.

Any intention is the "what you want to result from the spell" part of practicing magick. And, sure it sounds like it would be obvious. "If I perform a money spell, then I must want money." But do you? Is that what you mean? There are three good reasons to set intentions.

First, you want to set an intention so your desires are clearly communicated. Remember, you are powering your spell with this intention, so you need to send out this intention into the universe. No intention behind a spell is the same as just performing a scene from a play.

Secondly, setting a clear and concise intention will guarantee that you do not manifest something that you do not actually want, or that you manifest something in a detrimental way. For example, let's say you want to be able to quit your current job and go into business for yourself, but to make that transition you will need money. So, you set the desire, "I desire money. I WILL have enough for all of my desires." At first glance, that makes sense. You need money, so you ask for money. A short time later, you get called into your boss' office and they give you a substantial raise (with additional responsibilities). Although you will now have enough money to start your own business, you will need to continue to work for your employer to receive it, plus you now feel beholden to your employer for giving you such a raise. It turns out that you are actually *further* from reaching your desire of becoming an entrepreneur. That is because your intention was not clear and concise. You thought you just needed money, but that was not correct. Perhaps changing your intention to, "I desire to work for myself doing what I love while it brings me financial abundance month after month" would be the more specific and true intention. That is what you actually want, so ask for it.

The final reason to set an intention is for power. As we have discussed, the fuel behind sending your intention into the universe is the intention. So how strong do you want your spell to be? You won't overpower the universe, so give it everything you have! Once you have that clear and concise intention in your mind, harness and use that power by making sure all your thoughts and feelings support your intention.

Sacred Space for Practice

For many practitioners, there is inherent magick to be found in having a sacred space to practice. In setting this space, you are not only setting up a physical space, but also a space where the physical plane meets the spiritual plane. The space that you choose for yourself can either be a permanent sacred space specifically set aside for your practice, or it can be a temporary space that you set up each time you practice or during months that you are able to be outside. It can be inside your home or it can be outside among nature. It really is up to you when it comes to where you practice and what you make your sacred space. There are a few tips on choosing and creating your sacred space.

- Take your time and choose wisely.
  - Just because you happen to have a spare corner in your basement, does not necessarily mean that is where you want to practice your Wicca or witchcraft. You will want to choose somewhere that makes you feel welcome, comfortable, and peaceful. Right there beside the furnace may not be a great choice! Outdoor sacred space can be perfect and powerful but keep inclement weather in mind. You may either need a backup plan for those rainy days or, like me, you may only be able to use an outside space a few months per year and be inside the remainder of the year.

Personally, I keep a "permanent" sacred space inside my home but create a "temporary" sacred space in a nearby forest whenever the weather cooperates. Also, consider lighting conditions, foot traffic, noise, etc.

- Make it your own.
  - Customize the space to yourself or your intention. This space is for *you* and it should reflect *you*. Perhaps you have decided to use your college student's now spare bedroom. Then down come the puppy posters and the mirror with band stickers all over it. Give it a cleaning. Hang some of your things on the walls, put some of your books and knickknacks on the shelves, hang that painting of the Green Man that caught your eye. Bring in your straight-backed chair for meditation. Add a small table you can use as an altar or workspace. Don't forget your candles and some colored scarves. Whatever you need to do to make the space feel like it is yours and yours alone.

- Cleanse the space.
  - Once you have chosen your space and redecorated it to amplify your personality, you will want to perform a ritual cleansing of your new sacred space. This will eliminate negativity or evil that may be remaining in the area. This is a very important step in preparing your sacred space. There is nothing that will cause more unwanted or dangerous repercussions to your magick than having evil within your work area. Negativity will attach itself to your intentions anytime it possibly can and, at the very least, nullify any positivity you are attempting to manifest. At most, it can literally change a spell with pure intention into a manifestation of evil. When you are using a permanent installation of sacred space, you should cleanse through smudging at least once per month. Also, for this type of sacred space, consider performing a simple incantation in order to clarify your intent to dedicate this space to the practice of white magick and banishing all negativity and

evil from the space. If you are setting up a temporary sacred space, smudge every time you set up your space.

After you have chosen a sacred space, made it yours, and cleansed it of negativity, you will need an altar. Don't panic, it is not as difficult to prepare as it sounds. Let's explore altars and see just what you will need.

ALTARS

Just as with a sacred space, some Wicca and witchcraft practitioners have the ability to maintain a permanent altar, while others choose the temporary option. Truthfully, it depends on your circumstances, your available space, and your location.

Altars are available through Wicca supply stores, but they are not truly an item that is necessary to purchase as opposed to making your own. Pretty much any flat surface can be used as an altar (a table, a desk, a coffee table...). The only caveat to altars I would offer is that it be made of a natural material like wood, stone, concrete, or glass. Synthetic materials, although easier to find, are just not as conductive to energy transfer as natural materials. Personally, my inside altar is a table made of repurposed pallet wood and my outside, natural altar is a tree stump found in the forest behind my home.

Altars can be decorated in whichever way you prefer. Perhaps try some colorful scarves to match the intent of the spell or ritual you will be performing, or the time of year you are performing your ritual. Maybe you would like to scatter some flower petals on the altar to signify spring or some colorful leaves when autumn is in full bloom. Feel free to place some of your favorite crystals on the altar, just be sure that the crystals have been cleansed.

The most important items on your altar will be your tools. We will be covering the necessary tools in the next section. Just know that on your altar, you will need to leave a comfortable amount of room for the appropriate tools.

The only person who needs to like your altar is you. So never feel as if you would be performing better magick with a fancier altar. The altar is meant to celebrate what you have been given through nature, thank the God and Goddess for your blessings, and help to reflect your intentions into the universe. Nowhere in that list is the altar to show how much spending power you wield. Nature has no use for money so you will never gain favor from a tree spirit simply by having LED lights around your chalice. Make your altar reflect your intention and your commitment to the God and Goddess and you cannot possibly go wrong.

Basic Tools for Witchcraft - The Witch's Toolkit

The Cauldron

The witch's cauldron is a very recognizable iconic symbol that even people outside of Wicca or witchcraft are familiar with and will recognize. In Wiccan traditions, the cauldron is a symbol of creation and transformation, as well as fire. It is a sacred tool to the Goddess due to its shape and symbology of creativity and transformation. It can be used in a number of different ways during your practice. Because cauldrons are metal, they are excellent for use in fire spells, as incense holders, as a place to burn candles until completely consumed, or as a place to make and burn charcoal. Don't worry, you won't be making soup, even though the word "cauldron" automatically draws forth the vision of mysterious ingredients in a witch's broth. Actually, the roots of that pop culture fallacy are traceable back to none other than William Shakespeare!

> *"Double, double toil and trouble;*
> *Fire burn and cauldron bubble.*
> *Fillet of a fenny snake,*
> *In the cauldron boil and bake;*
> *Eye of newt and toe of frog,*
> *Wool of bat and tongue of dog,*
> *Adder's fork and blind-worm's sting,*
> *Lizard's leg and howlet's wing,*
> *For a charm of powerful trouble,*
> *Like a hell-broth boil and bubble."*
> - William Shakespeare (from Macbeth)

Cauldrons are, unfortunately, quite expensive and can vary greatly in size. However, the thought of the huge cauldron hanging over the open fire is really unnecessary. Those were literally cooking vessels and are not exactly in fashion in the modern world. So, if you are able to afford a small cauldron for your altar, wonderful! If you have a difficult time convincing yourself that a cauldron is a necessary expense, like me, feel free to use a sturdy and thick metal bowl. It will fill the role just fine.

The Elements

Traditionally, and in the vast majority of practices, there are four elements that are focused on in Wicca. The four elements are earth, air, fire, and water. Each of the elements are associated with cardinal directions, traits, as well as being guardian beings invoked for protection when casting a sacred circle.

The following cardinal directions are for the northern hemisphere. If you are in the southern hemisphere, use the opposite cardinal direction.

Earth - The element of earth is fertile and stable. The earth is considered the ultimate feminine element and is associated with the Goddess. The earth is circular and, as the Wheel of the Year turns, we are able to watch the seasons change and we watch the cycle of life play out because of it: birth, life, death, and rebirth. The earth is nurturing and stable, solid and firm, full of endurance and strength. Earth's cardinal direction is north.

Air - The element of air is connected to the soul, breath of life, and communication. Air carries away our strife and troubles and, as such, is associated with positive thoughts and peace. It is a good element to focus on if your spell deals with wisdom or powers of the mind. Air's cardinal direction is east.

Fire - The element of fire is connected to both creation and destruction. Fire is purifying with a masculine energy connected to strong will and is associated with the God. Fire's cardinal direction is south.

Water - Water is used for healing, cleansing, and purification. It is associated with passion and emotion. Water is used and sacred in many world religions, and Wicca is no different. "Holy Water" is saltwater that has been blessed by a long-time practitioner of the faith. Some Wiccan covens use their own holy water to consecrate the circle and tools used in spell work and rituals. Water's cardinal direction is west.

There are some modern traditions that include a fifth element - that of spirit. Spirit is also sometimes referred to as Akasha or Aether. The spirit element acts as a bridge between the physical plane and the spiritual plane.

Just like everything in the Wiccan belief, how much you incorporate the elements is completely your choice. However, it is important to keep in mind that the elements are used as a foundation in the vast majority of Wiccan and witchcraft spell work that you will come across in your reading and research.

The Chalice

The chalice is also sometimes referred to as a "goblet". Traditionally, the chalice is silver, and its use depends upon the spell or ritual being performed. It can contain wine, ale, water, or remain empty (to be symbolically filled during the ritual). The chalice is considered a tool of femininity and represents the Goddess, the element of water, and is a not-so-subtle symbol of fertility.

Although the chalice is not a Wiccan "necessity", it is a tool that I highly recommend for its powerful symbolism and its versatility.

Incense and Smoke

Incense has been used by every religion dating back to antiquity. The smoke of incense is associated with the spiritual world. It also is the only tool that represents two of the four elements - those are the elements of air and fire. Incense is a core component of every Wiccan ritual and in the practice of magick.

Incense is available in a seemingly unending number of scents, however, the scent is secondary in its use of magic. The more important portion of incense for our uses is the smoke itself which has the symbolic ability to carry our desires into the universe under the power of our intent. It is even possible to learn how to create your own incense with customized scents.

Traditionally, incense was used in witchcraft rituals by placing a blend of dried herbs in a censer or cauldron. However, in modern practice, most use either incense sticks or cones because they are inexpensive, and gathering your own herbs and charcoal is time-consuming.

The Candles

Since humans have learned to create lasting light, we have been using candles. Candles are now used as a major part of every Wiccan and witchcraft ritual. Simply put, no Wiccan gathering is complete without candles.

In each sacred circle, the cardinal directions are marked with specifically colored candles – Green or brown for the north, yellow or white for the east, red or orange for the south, and blue for the west. Also, on the altar would be 2 pillar candles to represent the God and the Goddess.

Within different spells, any number of candles may be lit and extinguished during the spell work.

The mere act of lighting a candle can be a powerful expression or energetic doorway-opener of intention. It can make a strong and deep connection between you and the magick which you are attempting to manifest. They are great for focus and meditation as well.

The Crystals and Stones

Each crystal and stone have unique properties which make it useful in different types of magick. Some are good for protection and grounding, while others excel at enhancing the connection between the practitioner and the spirit realm.

We will only be exploring a few of the thousands of stones and crystals which hold magickal significance because there are thousands of reference books out there dedicated solely to the subject. However, we should have a working knowledge of the following stones and crystals.

- Black Tourmaline

- Black Tourmaline is a power healer and protector crystal. Specifically, it is useful in blocking psychic attacks and negative thought patterns. It is even used as protection against harmful electromagnetic radiation caused by modern electronics.

- Black Obsidian

- Black Obsidian is formed when molten lava is cooled very quickly, like when it comes into contact with water. It works wonderfully as a protective shield against negativity and evil. It soaks up bad energy like a sponge and holds it. Because of its retention ability, you will want to cleanse your obsidian regularly by simply holding it under running water and visualizing all of the negativity washing from the stone, down the drain, and out of your life.

- Selenite

- Selenite has been a favorite among crystal lovers dating back to Ancient Greece. Some Greeks actually made windows from thin slabs of Selenite. It is found deep in the caves of Mexico, Morocco, and Madagascar, and the raw crystal formations in the caves can reach up to 35 feet long. The caves are absolutely beautiful, assuming you would find Superman's Fortress of Solitude to be beautiful! Selenite is very useful in cleansing and clearing a home or office because it dispels negative energy and creates calm in any space. Selenite lamps are also a great alternative to Himalayan salt lamps because it not only looks great when lit but is also self-cleansing and can cleanse other crystals in its environment.

- Amethyst

- Amethyst has been used since the middle ages as a healing crystal. It is widely used for its ability to protect its bearer emotionally and spiritually by helping to break anxious or addictive thought patterns and ties to stressful energies. Also, a piece of amethyst on your nightstand or under your pillow can help protect you from nightmares.

– Carnelian

- Carnelian is an absolutely beautiful, polished stone with swirls of red, orange, and brown. It is a great way to stay energized but calm at the same time. It will keep you grounded even when the atmosphere around you is buzzing. Carnelian can make you feel comfortable without the effects of laziness or complacency.

– Clear Quartz

- Clear quartz is an extremely dynamic and versatile crystal. It is useful in both deflecting negativity and attracting positivity. Also, clear quartz is easily able to pick up and funnel intention. Just as it does in its use in laser functionality, in television projection tubes and in early computer motherboards, clear quartz is a ready-made energy storage and amplification device.

- Smoky Quartz

- This opaque gray crystal is a personal favorite. Smoky Quartz helps you in manifesting your desires out of the ethereal plane and into the material world. But the beautiful part is that, once you have made your ideas into reality, smoky quartz will also protect those intentions from any evil or negative energies that may attempt to get in the way.

- Black Jade

- Black jade can help you stay clear of negative people and situations by helping you tune into the root source of the negativity. Sometimes it is just easier to avoid contact with negativity than it is to try to rid yourself of it. Black Jade is also known to assist you in tapping into your intuition.

- **Smithsonite**
  - Smithsonite is a soothing stone that can help calm your emotions and connect you to your center. Having a calm mind and a grounded center is absolutely vital to the success of many of the spells, rituals, and prayers we have discussed. Plus, who couldn't use some help relaxing after a stressful day or event!

- **Limestone**
  - Any witch who already practices, or spiritualist familiar with crystals, is undoubtedly confused by this addition. Limestone is not usually included in a list of stones or crystals used in any kind of spell work. However, limestone is very special. Limestone is found as bedrock in non-sandy environments and is often used to build the foundation of many of the homes in these non-sandy environments. And a special quality of this common stone is that it contains natural clear quartz and silica. Within the metaphysics community, limestone is seen as a storage vessel for energy. There is also

the paranormal theory that limestone allows for storage and release of high-energy situations (the stone tape theory). For these reasons, I always include a piece of limestone with me during a cleansing session, and keep one nearby during meditation.

The Crystal Ball

The crystal ball is an iconic image of witchcraft, and of the psychic abilities associated with witchcraft. The crystal ball is used in the divination practice of scrying. We talked about scrying in Chapter 1.

I keep my crystal ball on my altar during rituals and spell work in order to keep it charged with magickal energy. Also, it seems to facilitate communication with the spiritual plane. In my opinion, the crystal ball acts as a two-way door, allowing the physical plane to access the spiritual plane and also giving the ethereal access to our world.

The Herbs

The use of herbs in magick is among the oldest practices in witchcraft. The earliest forms of "magick" was little more than an understanding of the health and aromatherapy benefits of natural herbs. Anything that the general public does not understand has always been considered "magick" or "supernatural". Modern Wicca and the practice of witchcraft has grown from those early times of healing. Now we have gained significantly more knowledge, experience, and a deeper understanding of the benefits of herbs and herbal remedies.

In the practice of magick, herbs can be used in three different forms - fresh, dried, or oil. Fresh and dried herbs are self-explanatory. An herb oil can be made by infusing either coconut oil or olive oil with an herb. Add the herb to the oil, allow it to sit for up to 48 hours, remove and discard the herb, and cover the oil for future use.

There is a world of herbs. A discussion of each and every herb would take volumes of encyclopedia-sized books. So instead of getting into all herbs, we are going to focus on a handful of herbs that are the most commonly used in magick.

– Basil

- Basil has been used for hundreds of years as a spice in the Mediterranean, and most people would have basil in their kitchen. The magickal properties of basil include love, wealth, purification, and the banishing of negative or evil spirits. Basil corresponds to the masculine energy and is associated with the element of fire.

Medically, basil is known to produce a mild sedative effect when consumed as a tea. The essential oil produced from basil displays natural anti-fungal and antibiotic properties.

– Bay Leaf

- Commonly used as a spice in culinary recipes, bay leaf grows as a shrub with shiny leaves. Medicinally, bay leaf is used for relieving symptoms of the common cold, and treatment of headaches. The essential oil produced from bay leaf is used as a treatment for arthritis and sore muscles.

– Burdock
  - Burdock is associated with the element of water. Burdock has feminine energy and is used during rituals to protect the practitioner against negative energy, for healing, and for protection in general.

– Chamomile
  - Chamomile is probably best known as a calming tea, but when growing it produces beautiful daisy-like flowers. The magickal properties of chamomile include purification, protection, meditation, and luck with love and money. Chamomile corresponds to the masculine energy and is associated with the element of water.

- Cinnamon
- Cinnamon is a spice with a rich history. Its origins can be found as an Asian evergreen tree with the spice produced from

the bark. The cinnamon tree also produces flowers and berries that are still used in Eastern medicine today. Cinnamon can be used for protection, luck, love and passion, healing, and economic prosperity.

− Coltsfoot

- Coltsfoot is the first flowering plant that appears at the beginning of the growing season, often as early as February. It is a useful herb for springtime rituals, such as Imbolc, Ostara, and Beltane. Coltsfoot is connected to love, tranquility, and money. It is associated with the element of water.

− Comfrey

- Although Comfrey is lesser-known in modern times, it has been used for treating skin conditions for over 2,000 years. The magical properties of comfrey include healing, protection of travelers, protection against theft, good luck, and cleansing. Comfrey corresponds to the feminine energy and is associated with the element of water.

- **Dandelion**
  - Even though this flower is often considered a weed, it is not widely known that it is an edible flower and has been traditionally used in spring salads, teas, and in wine. The magickal properties of dandelion include purification, relaxation, and a return to child-like innocence.

- **Lavender**
  - The fragrant purple flower of this herb is well known and is used in perfumes, soaps, and oils. The magickal properties of lavender include cleansing, luck, evoking spirits and entities, happiness, and rejuvenating sleep. Lavender corresponds to the masculine energy and is associated with the element of air.

- **Mint**
  - Mint is not just for mojitos anymore! If you are growing your own herbal garden, mint should be grown in a container because it will spread and can easily take over your entire garden. There are also many different

varieties of mint, so you should research which variety would work best depending on the form you plan to use (fresh, dried, or oil). The magickal properties of mint include wealth, luck, healing, and protection. Mint corresponds to the feminine energy and is associated with the element of earth.

- **Oregano**
  - Oregano is an ancient spice which we are all familiar with through its uses in food preparation. However, the magickal properties include happiness, tranquility, harmony, and spiritual growth. Oregano corresponds to the feminine energy and is associated with the element of air.

- **Red Hibiscus**
  - Hibiscus is a beautiful and sweet-smelling flowering decorative plant. Magickly, red hibiscus is associated with love and lust.

- **Rosemary**
  - This herb is the most commonly used in ritual and spell work. The magickal properties include protection, cleansing, courage, and knowledge. Rosemary corresponds to the masculine energy and is associated with the element of fire.

- **Rue**
  - Rue is a very strong and useful herb that will help to banish negativity from your life. Rue can be sprinkled around the outside of your home to ward it against negative influences and entities, or added to a magickal bath to cleanse yourself of negative thoughts and to help in breaking bad habits. Spell bags made with rue will help in breaking malicious spells and magick and help to protect you from further interference.

- **Sage**
  - The indigenous people of North America have been harvesting sage for thousands of years. The magickal properties of sage include wealth, purification, good health, wisdom, and

protection. Sage corresponds to the masculine energy and is associated with the element of air.

- **St. John's Wort**
  - St. John's Wort is an extremely versatile and powerful herb. I would go so far as to call it a "must-have" for any Wiccan or practitioner of witchcraft. When used in a spell bag or sachet, St. John's Wort will help you in overcoming challenges, find that hidden pocket of personal courage, keep you moving forward through difficult times, increase your divination success, help you develop your psychic abilities, as well as protect you from negative magic and malevolent entities. Placing a sachet of St. John's Wort under your pillow at night can trigger prophetic dreams. Further, storing your St. John's Wort near your divination tools will help to cleanse them of negativity and increase your connection with the tools.

- **Thyme**
  - One of the first recorded uses of thyme is in the Egyptian mummification process, even before it was recorded being used as a food spice. The magickal properties of thyme include healing, courage, attraction, and the enhancement of psychic abilities. Thyme corresponds to the feminine energy and is associated with the element of water.

- **Valerian**
  - Valerian root has been used medicinally for at least the past 500 years. It has been described as having a sedative effect similar to the modern class of drugs known as benzodiazepines. The magickal properties of valerian include love, protection, mending of relationships, and restoration. Valerian corresponds to the feminine energy and is associated with the element of water.

The Pentacle

The pentacle is undoubtedly the most commonly misunderstood symbol and tool of Wicca. The pentacle is an _upright_ five-pointed star inside a circle, along with eight holy symbols (meant to symbolize the drawing together of the four elements and the divine). Many mistake the pentacle for the satanic pentagram. A pentagram is an _upside-down_ five-pointed star inside a circle (meant to draw together the elements and the power of Satan from below). Remember - up to raise yourself, down to lower yourself.

The pentacle is usually placed in the center of the altar and items to be consecrated are placed upon it, in order to offer assurance and power in your magickal works.

The Wand

As cliche as it may sound, the wand is actually a very important tool for the male witch. The wand replaces the besom, or broom, of a female witch.

A wand can be made of any natural material, however wood is the most common. It is used for the stabilization of energy within a coven. It is an obviously phallic representation and is associated with masculinity, vitality, strength, and virility. The wand is associated with the elements of air and fire, depending upon the type of spell work or ritual being performed.

In its docile form, the wand is used to represent power, will, and intent. The wand is especially useful in sanctifying a hallowed space or in the conjuring of spirits.

The Tarot

As with the crystal ball, the tarot card deck is a tool of divination. In the hands of someone who does not understand the meaning behind the cards, a tarot deck is little more than a collection of pictures. However, if the reader has taken the time to learn to develop their ability, the tarot deck can be a powerful tool of guidance and self-discovery.

The Besom

The besom is a straw broom, either full-sized or more the size of a feather duster. It is used to "sweep" a ceremonial or ritualistic space, clearing out and expelling any negative energy which may be present.

The besom is associated with femininity. The besom signifies a purifier and is associated with the element of water. Within the toolkit of a male Wiccan or witch, the besom may be replaced with the wand.

The Athame

An athame is a dagger-style, double-edged knife. The handle of the athame is traditionally made of a dark wood, however I have seen some beautiful examples with handles made of shaped crystal. Some covens require both an athame and a separate sword, but more modern magickal practices have foregone the sword. The athame is used in the casting of the sacred circle. Because the athame is used to direct energy into the casting, it is quite important that the athame remain cleansed and that it is consistently charged with moonlight. An athame is usually held as one of a Wiccan's or witch's most personal and important tools. We are pouring such a large amount of our trust and power into the athame while casting a sacred circle, that the athame becomes a prized possession.

An athame is not used as a physical blade. It is not to be used to cut anything on the physical plane. This is magickal work taking place on the spiritual plane and it should be reserved for that use only.

STEP-BY-STEP GUIDES

Step-By-Step Guide to Creating an Altar

Your altar is your space to demonstrate devotion. It is your most personal space because it is the artistic expression of you, your magic, and your practices. An altar is a physical manifestation of your personal spiritual journey, a display of your internal magickal self.

There are no hard and fast rules for creating your altar, and it can easily be changed and updated as your practices grow by adding or taking items away.

1. The first step in creating an altar is finding an appropriate placement. An altar can be inside your home or outside amongst nature. For obvious reasons, it is preferable to make your altar in a natural setting. But, for the majority of us, that is just not an option due to climate or access to forest land. As such, the majority of modern altars are made inside of our homes.

You will want to choose a location inside your home with minimal traffic. This is a sacred personal space meant to reflect you and you alone. It should be a place where you can feel completely safe and open to meditation, concentration, and communication with the spirit plane.

2. Next, you will choose the physical object which will be the altar. This object can be any flat surface made of a natural material

- a table, a bookshelf, a coffee table, a large cardboard box, etc.

3. Use some colored fabric (I use different colored scarves, some with patterns, some with symbols) to cover the top of the altar. The colors can represent the type of spell work you will be performing, or the ritual you will be performing, or the season, or the deity associated with the work you will be performing. This fabric is the base of the energy or intent you are attempting to transmit into the universe.

4. Next, place your pentacle onto the altar. The pentacle is normally positioned in the horizontal center, and just above the vertical center, of the altar. From the time when the pentacle is placed on the altar, all tools or items which should be consecrated should be touched to the pentacle prior to being placed on the altar.

5. The next step is to place your tools on the altar, first touching the tool to the pentacle for purification and symbolic devotion of the item to the magick to be practiced. The location of each tool is completely up to your personal wishes.

6. Lastly comes the placement of two pillar candles on the altar to represent the God and Goddess. White is always a good choice for these candles as it symbolizes purity, but I have also seen a green candle for the God and a blue candle for the Goddess, or an orange candle for the God and a black candle for the Goddess (day and night).

Step-By-Step Guide to Spell or Ritual Preparation

Properly preparing for spell work or a ritual is vital. Once the doorway is opened, you do not want to be shrouded in doubts, negativity, or uncertainty.

1. Get clear with your intentions. As we have discussed, knowing what it is that you actually desire is crucial in getting the results you want.

2. Words are important. Misspeaking, mispronouncing, or forgetting a section of language can be very detrimental to your spell or ritual, and could actually be quite dangerous spiritually in the case of names (the names of angels and demons can be very similar, on purpose some would say). If you are not reading directly from a spellbook, it is a good idea to write the wording down. Better yet, write the entire spell or ritual into your grimoire (magickal journal) so that you can then note any effects which were seen.

3. Be clean when stepping onto the astral plane. Prior to beginning your spell or ritual, take the time to cleanse your physical being with protection and to draw energy. If you can bathe, add some salt or a small sachet of herbs and salt to your bathwater. If showering, use a bit of salt as a scrub. It can help you feel more relaxed to know you have removed any negativity from yourself that may taint your magick.

4. Gather all of the ingredients you will need for your spell work or ritual. It may sound silly but trust me it happens. You are halfway through a spell and realize you left the rosemary on the kitchen table! Been there, done that. So, check and double-check that you have everything you will need at the ready.

Step-By-Step Guide to Casting A Circle

Casting a circle is the beginning of any session of spell work or ritual. The circle serves two purposes - as a doorway to the spiritual plane, and as a protective barrier keeping the practitioner safe from evil while performing the spell work or ritual. Think of it as a tunnel connecting your spiritual self (your energy which is tethered to your body) with the spiritual plane. Opening the circle is crucial to your magickal being and closing the circle upon completion of your spell work or ritual is crucial to your physical being.

You need to cast a circle **every time** you are going to perform a spell or a ritual, no matter how little or gigantic the energy output or the time involved in the work. Practicing while not in a circle can lead to demonic attachments, negative soul ties, or possibly unleashing something even older and more evil than a demon. When we practice without a circle, we make *ourselves* the doorway into the spiritual plain and there is no telling what may walk through that doorway. We need not approach magick or the spiritual plain with fear, but with respect. In the words of Friedrich Nietzsche,

> "*He who fights with monsters might take care lest he thereby become a monster. And if you gaze for long into the abyss, the abyss gazes also into you.*"
> -Nietzsche

1. Establish the amount of space you will need for your ritual or spell. For a single person, a good rule of thumb is to stretch your arms straight out from your sides, mark those points. Then from those points, take one large step away from the center. This will be the outer marks to cast your circle.

The point is to have a circle that is small enough as to be easy to cast and control, but not so small that you end up stepping outside the circle at any time during your spell or ritual. Once the circle is cast, do not step or reach over the boundary line.

"Breaking" the circle can, and does, result in the same negativity and attachments as performing magick without a circle. Should something occur and you must exit the circle prior to closing it: visualize a door through the edge of the circle, open the door, walkthrough, close the door behind you. It is only as strong as your ability to visualize, so it is certainly not ideal.

2. Next, you will need to cleanse your circle of any negative energy or entities which may be present. This can be done by ritually sweeping them outside of the circle using the besom, ordering them out using the wand, burning incense, or sprinkling saltwater within the circle. Whichever method you choose, visualize the negative energy dispersing from the sacred space as you perform the ritual.

3. If you are practicing outside among nature, the physical circle can be drawn using your athame by either carving in the soil or by symbolically tracing the circle. If you are casting the circle in your home, you can either use salt poured over the athame or by symbolically tracing the circle. However, if

116

merely tracing the circle, be cautious that you remember the outline so as not to prematurely break the circle prior to closing. Either way, you would walk clockwise (known as "sunwise" in Wiccan and witchcraft traditions) starting at the eastern point of the circle. As you make your transits, visualize that you are pouring out energy, power, and protection into the barrier. Personally, I visualize each transit adding blue flaming rings which reach up and disappear into the sky above me.

4. You will want to make a number of complete transits. I suggest either 3, 6, or 9 transits as they are strong protective numbers in numerology. As you reach each cardinal direction point, call it out and, if you are using crystals or other markers to signify the directions, place your marker down on the first transit. To call out the cardinal directions, use the following words:

"I call upon the energy of the (north, east, south, or west). Welcome to this circle of light. Join in my magick. So mote it be."

When your transits are complete and you feel that you have created a space that feels healthy and balanced, the circle casting ritual is complete.

Step-By-Step Guide to Rituals

Wouldn't it be wonderful if I could just write down exactly how to perform every ritual! Alas, that is not how the practice of Wicca and witchcraft works. There is an endless number of rituals one can perform or participate in, and an endless number of ways to perform or participate in each one. Most likely, the first ritual a beginner Wiccan or practitioner of witchcraft will perform should be a dedication ritual, dedicating oneself to Wicca and to the God and Goddess. A dedication ritual would be performed as follows:

1. Cast a protective circle.

2. Light a candle representing the God, a candle representing the Goddess (or candles representing your chosen deities), and a dedication candle representing your intention. The deity candles can be extinguished following the ritual, but the dedication candle should be left to burn out on its own.

3. Light an incense to carry your intention to the spiritual realm.

4. The language recited should be similar to the following:

"I call upon the power of the God and of the Goddess (or Universe, Angels, Spirit, Ascended Masters, Protectors, etc.). It is my intention to dedicate myself to you and your praise. I will follow the Wiccan Rede and ask that you, in return, bless my magick and my life with your light and power; keep me safe physically, mentally, emotionally, and spiritually throughout my journey. All the many splendors of nature bow to you, as do I. Thank you for the blessings you have and will pour out onto me. My devotion is yours. So mote it be!"

Step-By-Step Guide to Closing A Circle

When your magickal session or ritual is finished, you will need to close the circle. Closing the circle will close the doorway you have opened to the spiritual plane and signify that you have finished your work, allowing your intentions to be dispersed.

1. Begin by addressing each element of earth, air, fire, and water. As an example, I use the language:

"Thank you to the earth element which grounds me. Thank you to the air element which blows me forward on my journey. Thank you for the fire element which lights my way. Thank you to the water element which cleanses and purifies me and my works."

2. A thank you should be expressed to the God and Goddess for lending their power to your magick or ritual.

3. Beginning again in the east and walking counter-clockwise (or "moonwise"), make the same number of transits around the circle as you did at the casting. This time, visualize the power and energy returning to you.

4. When you have reached the eastern point after the correct number of transits, end the session with, *"So mote it be!"*

Step-By-Step Guide to Crystal Magick

As we discussed earlier, there are simply too many different crystals to provide an exhaustive list within this book. However, crystal magick is extremely powerful and useful to all Wiccan and witchcraft practitioners. Because of the power and popularity of crystal magick in modern Wicca, It would be remiss if we did not at least cover some basics of the practice.

Having the proper crystals present at the time of a spell or ritual is like running your magick through a spiritual amplifier. The crystal will focus the magical energy, add additional correspondences to strengthen the work, and store magickal energy for future use.

Crystals are also used in holistic healing practices. The theory behind the use of crystals is one of vibrational frequency.

Everything in nature has a vibrational frequency, including you and me. The higher the vibrational frequency, the closer the object is to the spiritual plane. Crystals have been shown to have extremely high vibrational frequency. This property is what allows for enhanced communication between the two planes when using crystal magick. Crystals placed on the body, in the area of disease or pain, can raise the vibrational frequency of that area and the surrounding aura, leading to faster and more comprehensive healing. In my opinion, it is also this property that makes modern cancer treatments even slightly effective. When delivering radiation therapy, doctors pass radioactive isotopes between two neodymium magnets and then through a quartz crystal which focuses the isotopes into a laser-like beam. I believe that they could actually focus non-radioactive, magnetized materials through a quartz crystal and get the same result. It is not the poisonous radiation that is causing the healing, but the higher frequency of the ions after passing through the quartz crystal.

The first thing that you must do when you buy or receive a new crystal is to cleanse it and power it with your personal magick and light.

Your crystal may have been dug from the ground or grown under controlled conditions. Following that, it most likely went through some sort of tumbling and polishing process. Then it was sold to a wholesale crystal company, who then likely sold it to a pagan, new age, or Wiccan supply shop (or even Amazon!). It sat in this shop for an undetermined amount of time until being selected by you and taken into your home. Throughout this entire process, your new crystal has been absorbing energies of people who came into contact with it or were even in its immediate vicinity. How sure are you that each of these people was positive, enlightened, upbeat people with no negative or evil attachments? Exactly. And that is why we need to immediately cleanse every new crystal.

To cleanse your crystal, I would recommend one of two methods. You can cleanse your crystal by holding it under running water for several minutes. In this method, you will want to visualize all of the negativity absorbed by the crystal being purged from inside the crystal and being washed down the drain or down the stream. The other method is to place your new crystal in salt for a few days. Much like you put your wet cellphone in rice to leech out water, placing your crystal into salt will leech out any negativity which it may have absorbed. Place the salt and crystal in an airtight container and keep it in a dark, cool location. After three-four days, you can retrieve your crystal and dispose of the salt. Do NOT consume this salt or use it as protection in any way. It is tainted with negativity and evil. Dispose of it immediately either in your trash can or by burial. Also, it is a good practice to cleanse your crystals and reset their intent at least once per month. Crystals pick up negativity like sponges (keeping it from you) and they can become evil-logged over time. Yes "evil-logged". I just created that word, but you knew exactly what I meant!

Once cleansed, it is time to imbue your crystal with your personal magick and light. This is accomplished simply by holding your crystal in your hands and focusing a meditative 5 or so minutes on directing your power, your intent, and your light into the crystal. A crystal should be an extension, a link between its owner and the spiritual plain. The more you are reflected by your crystal, the stronger the link. You can customize your crystals while empowering them as well by saying out loud what your intention for each is (i.e., "You will be used for healing", or "You will be used for protection").

Next, it is time to charge your crystal. Just like a battery, your crystal needs to have power stored inside in order to function properly. To charge your crystal (or some refer to this process as "mounting your crystal"), place them either in direct sunlight for a minimum of five straight hours, or place them under the light of a new or full moon overnight.

Now your crystal is ready to use! Depending on the crystal and your intent, wear it as jewelry, put it in your pocket as a talisman, hold it while meditating as a palm stone, keep them in a safe place for use

in healing, place it near your bed
or under your pillow to facilitate
more peaceful sleep and positive
dreams, put it on your altar for
spell work… The uses are as
boundless as your desires and
imagination.

Step-By-Step Guide to Candle Magick

Candles have only been widely used
for magickal purposes since the
early 1800's. Prior to that period,
colored candles were simply too
expensive to be afforded by anyone
but the upper class. However, with
advances in candle-making
techniques and the discovery of new
coloring elements, colored candles
have become extremely popular and
among the cheapest types of magick
to practice. Today, candles can be
found in any color imaginable, in a
wide variety of sizes, made from
many different materials, with or
without fragrance, and in the shape
of pretty much anything your heart
desires.

Because many spells call for the
candle to be left to burn itself out
of the duration of the efficacy of
the spell, I tend to stick with

short to medium-sized candles made of natural materials such as beeswax for the majority of spells, even opting for votive candles for short-duration spells. I do suggest large candles as the representation of the God and Goddess, as they are the focal point of any Wiccan spell or ritual and should last the longest.

The colors of candles are meant to focus and reflect your intent, as every color has a different meaning and can influence a person's emotions. Scientifically speaking, color is perceived due to the frequency of the light wave reflected from an object to our eyes. So just as crystals emit higher frequencies of energy, colors are reflected at different frequencies. The concept of vibrational frequency can be found at every level of nature and colors are no exception.

To aid you on your first journey into candle magick, I have included this listing of basic colors and meanings. This is by no means exhaustive, as there are different shades to consider, whether herbs are included inside the candle, fragrances, etc.

Black - Black is not dangerous or evil. Black is the color perceived when the object absorbs all of the colors of the spectrum and reflects none. Therefore, black is excellent at absorbing negative energy, pulling it from the air around you. You can use this inherent property to protect yourself. or to repel, reverse, or banish negative and evil energy from your surroundings

Blue - Blue is a color of relaxation and tranquility. It is often used to heal and strengthen the mind during spell casting. It is also useful to encourage sleep, allowing your intention to sleep to flow into the candle before burning it for a few short minutes and then extinguishing it.

Brown - Brown is largely considered a color of nature, from the soil beneath our feet to the color of many animals. Brown is often used in conjunction with other colors in order to tie a spell to the natural world - influencing the physical world around you rather than another person or yourself.

Green - Green is a very versatile color. Foremost, it represents the

Earth element. Green also represents growth, fortune, prosperity, and success. It can also be used effectively in healing.

Gold - Gold is primarily associated with the God, the sun, and masculinity. Gold is fantastic at attracting knowledge or developing a power of influence.

Orange - Orange is energetic and attentive. Orange is a great attracter of energy, influence, intentions, or lost objects. It is positive, spiritual, and physical energy and is associated with being encouraging and allowing for clear thoughts.

Pink - Pink is about connection, be it love or friendship. It is nurturing, encouraging the art of communication. Pink is often found at marriage ceremonies as it fosters affection and romance through communication.

Silver - Silver is primarily associated with the Goddess, the moon, and celestial bodies, and femininity. Silver encourages goodness to overcome evil, encourages the use of intuition, and

129

encourages self-reflection through meditation.

Red - Red conveys passion and health and is associated with energy and vitality. Red bolsters the soul against corruption by negativity. It is closely associated with the element of fire and, as such, lends itself to representing burning desire, lust, and sexual passion.

White - White is pure and unifying. Its purity allows it to be used in virtually any context, though it is most commonly associated with truth and illumination. Primarily a defensive color, it can also be used as a replacement for any color you do not have on hand or if you are unsure which color to use. It will help to connect you with the spiritual plane and to prevent evil from taking you over.

Yellow - Yellow is associated with knowledge, discovery, and innovation. It is the perfect color to use when studying any subject because it will help you to absorb the material and make the necessary logical connections. Yellow is also representative of the fulfillment of your dreams.

Violet - Violet is power. It encourages prowess in the magickal world, the spiritual plane. You can think of violet as magick steroids. Any spell you are casting or ritual you are performing will be magnified on the spiritual plane by incorporating violet. Casting a love spell? Burn a violet candle along with your pink candle to really bolster the effects of pink's affinity for love.

Choosing the proper candle for your needs does, of course, involve more than color. Candles can also vary greatly by size. Similar to other important aspects of life, it is not always a matter of "bigger is better", it depends on how it is used.

Many spells require that you allow a candle to burn itself out prior to either ending the spell or to move on to the next step of the spell or ritual. When you come across a long-duration spell, you may want a much larger candle. However, for short-duration spells and rituals, many use votives, short tapers, or menorah candles. Menorah candles are perfect for much of candle magic because they are readily available at any local grocery store, they are white and unscented, and they are short enough to be confident that they will burn themselves out in a reasonable amount of time.

Something to remember is that we cannot re-use leftover candles or candles that have been extinguished during other spell work. Once a candle is charged, impregnated with your intent and lit, its use is set. While burning, a candle may attract and hold negativity or evil. We would not remove bubble gum from our mouth, use it to clean dirt from the bottom of our shoe, and then pop it back into our mouth! Once we have begun to chew the gum, its use is set. It is the same concept. So always use fresh, or "virgin", materials in each spell work. This rule does not apply to the God or Goddess candle, as those candles are cleansed by their very intent.

Candles are also available in a variety of shapes or forms. They can be shaped as humans, animals, deities, etc. Here is just a short list of possible candle shapes and their uses.

Female Figure - This is used to attract or repel someone specific but can also be used to represent someone close to you who identifies as female.

Male Figure - This is used to attract or repel someone specific but can also be used to represent someone close to you who identifies as male.

Couple - Candles shaped like a couple are used to bring a married couple closer together.

Genitalia - This one is pretty obvious. It is used for arousal, passion, sexual desire, and fertility.

Buddha - This shape is often used to bring good fortune, abundance, and luck.

Devil - A devil-shaped candle is used for temptations, whether to encourage or banish them.

Cat - This shape is used specifically for money spells, luck spells, and for protection.

Skull - A candle shaped as a skull is used to repel unwanted feelings or thoughts. It is also used for healing and cleansing spells.

Knob - The seven knobs which make up the body of this candle shape represent seven wishes. Use them for what you desire.

Now that you have chosen your candle (the shape, the size, the color), how do you prepare the candle for use in spell work? Let's get into how we prepare candles for our magick.

1. Dress Your Candle - Imbuing your candle with your intent for the spell work is completed through the process of "dressing". Dressing your candle requires using a natural oil, such as grape seed oil. Apply the oil to the candle by rubbing it onto the candle from the top to the center point, then from the bottom to the center point.

2. Consecrate Your Candle - I actually combine the consecration of the candle with the dressing of the candle, instead of repeating a very similar process twice. To consecrate your candle, anoint the candle with a natural oil. While applying the oil, verbally dedicate the candle to your magick and to the purpose (intent) of the spell it will be used to facilitate.

At this point, your candle is ready to be used in your spell or ritual. The simplest spell in candle magick is one that simply carries your intent to the spiritual plane. It can be used for pretty much any manifestation-style desire.

Simple Candle Spell

You will need:

A prepared candle
A piece of paper and pen
A cauldron or metallic bowl

Steps:

1.   Cast a sacred circle.

2.   Light your prepared candle.

3.   Write your intended desire on a piece of paper.

4.   While reciting your intended desire aloud, light one corner

    of the paper on fire by holding
it in the flame of the
    candle.

5.   Place the burning paper into
the cauldron or metallic bowl
    and allow it to burn out
naturally.

There are also ways to "read" the
candle flame in order to ascertain
the strength of the spell and
spiritual energy being invested
into the manifestation of your
desire. It is a form of divination
related to spell efficacy. It can
certainly be helpful to have some
idea whether you might need to
repeat the spell or whether you
appear to have nailed it on the
first try. We will take a quick
glance into this spell-focused
divination.

High and Strong Flame –
Manifestation is proceeding
quickly.

Low and Weak Flame - There is a low
amount of spiritual energy invested
in your intentions. You may want to
begin preparations to repeat the
spell or ritual.

Thick Black Smoke - Active opposition exists to your work. This could mean that there are Wiccan or witchcraft practitioners actively casting negativity against you, or that your own subconscious mind is working against your intentions.

Dancing Flame - Indicates a highly energetic, but chaotic, manifestation.

Flickering Flame - Spirits are present within your circle and your prayers and intentions are being acknowledged.

Popping or Sputtering Flame - This signifies interference in the communication of your spell or ritual intent due to outside forces. It could be that something or someone is working against you, or that you may need to add more concentration and spiritual energy to your spell or ritual.

Flame Goes Out - A flame that suddenly extinguishes during your spell or ritual indicates that a stronger (more energetic) opposing force has ended your spell or ritual. You will need to deal with this negative force before you can be successful in the spell work or ritual.

Cannot Extinguish Flame - A flame that seems to refuse to be extinguished signifies that your work is not done. You should spend more time and invest more energy into the spell or ritual.

Step-By-Step Guide to Herb/Plant Magick

Herbal and plant magick is where the devotion to the Earth Mother or Goddess meets the art of nature. Wicca embraces the world of nature as a religion, and as we learn to cast spells and perform rituals, we invoke the energies and deities of nature to assist us on our path. It only makes sense that, as we worship all that nature brings, we also offer our devotion to the magick and healing abilities contained in the plants and herbs which support our practices. Because of this basic deeply rooted connection between herbs and Wicca, we would be hard-pressed to find a Wiccan or witch who does not use plants or herbs in their practices.

Plants and herbs offer our magick both a literal and an ethereal link to Mother Earth - growing from the minerals found in the soil, using the elements of earth, air, fire, and water. Even if the plants are grown using hydroponics, natural minerals must be included in the water in order for the plants to grow. Plants depend upon the wind to scatter their seeds in order to reproduce, not to mention their production of oxygen from carbon dioxide. They use the fire produced by the sun to provide their basic living function of photosynthesis. And plants use and store water in ways quite similar to those of animals. They are truly perfect examples of living in balance with the elements.

I am often asked about whether Wiccan and witchcraft practitioners must grow their own herbs for them to be effective in spell work or rituals. Simply put, the answer is "No". Is it better to grow the herbs and plants yourself? Absolutely. But store-bought herbs can be just as effective. Whether it is due to a lack of space, climate, or if, like me, your thumb is more black than green, sometimes it is just necessary that you buy the herbs you will be using. That is fine. Remember, it is the intent of the spell caster which gives power to a spell.

There are four forms in which we can use herbs in our magickal sessions – Raw, Sachets, Tinctures, or Elixirs. Each has its own pros and cons and some of the herbs limit their useful forms all on their own. The purpose and duration of the spell, along with the herb(s) being used, are all factors in the form best suited for use in the spell work or ritual.

Any herb or plant can be used in its **raw** form. In their raw state, herbs maintain their highest grounding energy. Further, some herbs are poisonous and cannot be ingested. Obviously, the raw form or sachet form are the only forms in which these herbs should be included in your spell work.

Sachets can be a convenient form of carrying bits of your magick with you throughout the day, much like an amulet or talisman. A sachet is a small cloth pouch containing the ingredients of a spell. They can be kept in a pocket, worn around your neck, tucked away in a purse, dangled from a rear-view mirror, floated in a cleansing bath, etc. Whether the herbs themselves are fresh or dried, a sachet can serve as the perfect vessel for maintaining the power of a spell near you for the duration of the magick.

A **tincture** is a naturally infused mixture of herbs, water, and alcohol. It is most often applied like a balm or salve and used in healing either the body, the mind, or the spirit. A tincture is created by placing the fresh or dried herbs in a glass jar, then adding equal parts water and alcohol (usually vodka or a high alcohol content rum). The jar is then sealed airtight and the mixture is left to steep for up to a month before use. When ready to use in the spell, the tincture is opened and the liquid and any solids which still remain are rubbed onto the skin as directed by the spell.

And finally, an **elixir**. Elixirs are made from herbs that can be safely ingested. They can be made and consumed as a tea, or steeped in a fashion similar to a tincture by steeping without heat. Most elixirs have the added ingredient of a natural sweetener to make them more palatable, such as honey or agave nectar.

CHAPTER 3 – CASTING SPELLS & RITUALS

Prosperity Spells

Money. The root of all... well... everything in modern society. At least on the physical plane. I get it. We all need money to pay rent, buy food, pay the electric bill, buy books on Wicca and witchcraft, etc. There are times when it may very well be necessary to use your magick to attract money. It can absolutely be done. I want to just throw out this caveat, do with it what you will.

Everything in magick has a give and take, everything has a yang to its yin. Do you see a large Wicca and witchcraft community in the world driving Porsches and wallpapering their homes with cash? There is a reason for that. Money has absolutely no spiritual value. Money is paper or, in our digital world, no more than a set of ones and zeros in a database. We do not want to waste our energies on things that do not bring us true joy or glorify the God or Goddess or beauty of the universe. Working on the spiritual plane to attract items that do not have any effect whatsoever on the spiritual plane can lead to mixed and, sometimes, undesired results. Perhaps it would make more sense to perform spell works that include specific wants or needs rather than the general "money" that many spell casters end up requesting. Try substituting money with "payment of my rent" or whatever it is that you truly desire.

MONEY CHARM BAG

This spell should be performed during a waxing crescent or full moon to lead to earthly success, abundance, and prosperity.

You will need:
- Incense: Use any scent associated with money (orange, cinnamon, etc.)
- A small bowl of salt
- A small bowl of water
- A red candle
- Basil (fresh or dried)

144

- Crystal: Any crystal associated with money (Citrine)
- Nail and hair clippings
- A silver coin from the year of your birth
- A token representing your work
- A small green pouch
- String

Instructions:

1. Cast a sacred circle.

2. Ground and center yourself.

3. Light the red candle and the incense.

4. Meditation and visualization play a vital role in this ritual. Meditate and visualize your life where the money you want is already with you.

5. Focus on every detail that you are visualizing, how you feel after getting the money that you need, how you are spending it and how it is affecting your life.

6. Take the basil into your hand and visualize yourself happy

and prosperous. Place the
basil into the pouch.

7. Take the crystal into your hand
and visualize that you are
holding the earth's agreement
to fulfill your desire. Place
the crystal into the pouch.

8. Take the nail and hair
clippings into your hand and
visualize yourself happy and
prosperous. Place the
clippings into the pouch.

9. Take the coin into your hand
and visualize yourself happy
and prosperous. Place the coin
into the pouch.

10. Take the token of work into
your hand and visualize
yourself happy and prosperous.
Place the object into the
pouch.

11. Close the pouch and tie it shut
with the string.

12. Pass the pouch through the
smoke of the incense. Pass the
pouch over the fire of the
candle. Sprinkle a pinch of the

salt onto the pouch. And splash
a bit of the water onto the
pouch.

13. Close the sacred circle. The
red candle should be allowed
to burn itself out.

13. Keep this pouch on a
windowsill, covered porch,
Greenhouse, somewhere that the
pouch will get both direct
sunlight and direct moonlight.

14. After the ritual's results
have manifested, or after 30
nights - whichever comes
first, open the bag and remove the
crystal. The bag should then
be re-tied and buried.

15. Do not forget to cleanse the
crystal before using it for
any other magickal or
spiritual purpose.

Money Oil

This potion can be used in any money
or prosperity spell, to dress
candles for instance. It can also
be used to anoint objects (like a
resume) or as a part of a ritual
bath (just a few drops is enough).

Its potency lasts for up to a year, so it is a good idea to just have some on hand when you need it.

The oil should be made during a waxing moon.

You will need:

- A jar with an airtight seal
- 3 whole cinnamon sticks (or the equivalent in dried spice form)
- Enough almond oil to fill the jar

Instructions:

1. Take a deep breath and intentionally remind yourself that your intent in making this oil is magickal.

2. Place the cinnamon sticks into the jar (breaking the sticks is fine if need be). If using dried spice, just pour the proper amount into the jar.

3. Fill the jar with the almond oil and seal it shut.

4. Shake the jar thoroughly.

5.   Keep the jar where it can receive direct sunlight.

6.   Shake the jar every two days.

7.   The oil will be ready when the moon returns to the same
     position it was when you began the preparation,
     approximately 4 weeks.

DOORSTEP BLESSING

This ritual will create a money-attracting herbal wash for your front door threshold. Because it will keep for years, it also makes a thoughtful and appreciated Yule gift for your Wiccan or witchcraft friends.

The mixture should be prepared on the first Thursday following a full moon and used on the first Thursday following a full moon.

You will need:

- A metal mixing bowl
- Fresh basil leaves
- Fresh dill

- A couple bills of large denomination (don't worry, these are not going anywhere)
- A handful of coins
- A saucepan
- White vinegar
- A jar with an airtight seal
- A small amount of Money Oil

Instructions:

1. Put the bills, coins, basil leaves, and dill into the
   mixing bowl.

2. Mix the ingredients together by hand. While mixing, recite
   the following: "The herbs herein are coated in money. Money
   is their nature. Success and money are drawn to these herbs
   as the moth is drawn to the flame."

3. Remove the bills. Place the remaining ingredients into the
   jar.

4. Bring the vinegar to a simmer in the saucepan. Then
   carefully pour it into the jar.

5.   Allow the jar to cool enough to touch.

6.   Seal the jar.

7.   Place your hand on the lid of the jar and recite the
        following:

> *"By the power of the Lady and Lord,*
> *By the power of my will and word,*
> *Money follow where you go,*
> *Money follow where you are,*
> *Money blessings at the door.*
> *So mote it be."*

8.   Use the Money Oil to mark a pentacle on the lid of the jar.

9.   Store the jar in a cool, dark place for one week.

10. After one week, the potion is ready to use.

11. To use the potion, wipe it onto the threshold of the most
        often used door to your home. As you do so, concentrate
        your energy on the abundance this potion will bring to you
        and your household.

12. You can renew the spell by rewashing the threshold every season. The shelf life of the potion is up to 5 years if kept sealed (other than for use) and stored in a cool and dark area.

SPELL FOR A GROWING PAY STUB

A pay stub is a physical representation of how much money our time is worth to our employer. We all believe that our time should be worth more than it is. So let's see how we can magickly grow our worth and watch the number on that pay stub increase!

This spell can be performed either outside in a garden or inside with a potted version. The location is not nearly as important as the time of year - late spring during a waxing moon.

You will need:

- A pay stub (or printout)
- A small amount of Money Oil
- A basil seedling

Instructions:

1.   Anoint the pay stub with Money
Oil. While doing so, recite
      the following:

      "This seedling shall grow,
      And my bank overflow.
      May the universe allow
      That I reap what I sow."

2.   Dig deep into the soil and
place the pay stub in the hole.

3.   Put some soil over the pay
stub.

4.   Plant the basil seedling on top
of the pay stub.

5.   Nurture and grow this plant
throughout the growing season.

PROSPERI-TEA

If you have any doubts about the
power of intention and clear
communication with the spiritual
plane, look no further than this
tea. This is a daily beverage of
thousands of individuals, but
without the directed intent and the
practice to communicate clearly

with the spiritual plane, it is not magickal in any fashion. The tea includes fresh tea leaves and bergamot. Fresh tea leaves and bergamot are also the ingredients of Earl Grey tea! Tea leaves and bergamot also both happen to be associated with wealth. Further, this tea is sweetened with honey - a natural substance associated with prosperity, long life, and good fortune.

Begin this spell on the first Thursday following a full moon and continue to make and drink one cup per day until the next full moon.

I do recommend that you buy the Earl Grey tea from a specialty shop or high-end market to ensure you are receiving the freshest and least processed tea. I also recommend that you source your honey so that it is as local and fresh as possible.

You will need:

- Earl Grey tea
- Honey

Instructions:

1.   Make a cup of tea. Sweeten it to taste with honey.

2.   Prior to your first sip, recite:

> "*I take abundance into me.*
> *Abundance comes to me.*
> *Through air, fire, water, earth.*
> *Abundance comes to me.*
> *So mote it be.*"

3.   Drink your cup of tea as you visualize yourself receiving the rewards you seek.

SPELL TO ATTRACT MONEY

You will need:
- Five candles (1 yellow, 1 white, 1 green, 1 red, and 1 blue)
- Hyacinth petals or oil
- Salt

Instructions:

1.   Dress the candles by rubbing them with the hyacinth petals or oil.

2.   Cast a sacred circle.

3. Inside the circle, draw a pentacle using the salt.

4. At each point of the pentacle, place one of the unlit
    candles.

5. Light each candle beginning with the upper point and
    proceeding clockwise (moonwise). As you light each candle,
    summon the power of the element represented by that
    candle's color. You can choose the order of the
    incantations by choosing the order of candles, but the
    incantations would be as follows:

"Through this yellow candle, I summon the power of the Air!

Through this green candle, I summon the power of the Earth!

Through this red candle, I summon the power of Fire!

Through this blue candle, I summon the power of Water!

Through this white candle, I summon the power of Spirit!"

6.   Stand in the center of the pentacle. Visualize energy from each of the colors flowing from the candles and joining your aura; your being.

7.   Recite the following incantation six times:

> *"With the powers of earth, air, fire, and water. With the power of spirit, you must hear my plea.*
>
> *It is money I need; money is my desire. I call upon God to grant this to me."*

8.   At the end of the sixth recitation, add *"So mote it be."*

9.   Allow the candles to burn themselves out.

10.   Close the sacred circle.

11.   Bury the candle remains.

SIMPLE CASH FLOW SPELL

This cash flow spell requires very few ingredients and a very short incantation. The true power of this spell comes from the visualization and our desire for money to mimic nature (an unending flow). The pink candle is used in this spell for its amplification power. This spell should be performed when the flow of moonlight is at its highest (a full moon).

You will need:

- A green candle
- A pink candle
- Small amount of patchouli oil

Instructions:

1. Dress the candles with patchouli oil.

2. Cast a sacred circle.

3. Stand at the center of the circle.

4. Ground and center your energy.

5. Visualize yourself standing in a free-flowing stream filled
     with shining coins and floating paper notes (bills). Focus
     until you can actually *feel* the excitement of being
     surrounded by this unending flow of cash.

6. As you hold onto that feeling, light the green candle and
     then thee pink candle.

7. Recite the following: *"With this fire, I summon the forces
     of nature and the elements. Money now flows to me from all
     sources. So mote it be."*

8. Allow the green and pink candles to burn themselves out.

9. Close the sacred circle.

SIMPLE MONEY SPELL

This simple money spell relies on your intention being carried to the spiritual plane. It is best performed on a new moon. With each successive night, as the moonlight grows more plentiful, so should your money.

You will need:
- 3 green candles in candle holders
- 3 one-dollar bills
- Either one or a blend of the following dried herbs: basil, cinnamon, clove, ginger, nutmeg, mint, dill, and patchouli

Instructions:

1.   Cast a sacred circle.

2.   Place the three-dollar bills on the ground, separated.

3.   Sprinkle the dried herb(s) onto each bill.

4.   Place one of the candles (in its holder) onto each bill.

5.   As you light each candle, recite the following: *"Money, fall down on me. Pour down on me in plenty. May I be wealthy and cause harm to no one."*

6.   Following the 3rd recitation, conclude it with *"So mote it be."*

7.   Close the sacred circle.

8.   Allow the three candles to burn themselves out.

Spells for Success

Aside from the simple acquisition of wealth and money, there is another way to achieve financial gain - being successful in your profession. The ability to encourage success, respect, and esteem in the workplace means not only being able to earn more money, but also leveraging your reputation in the marketplace to earn your true worth. For those who want to grow and improve their career, these spells and rituals offer a wonderful opportunity.

SPELL FOR SUCCESS

This spell can be useful in a number of professional circumstances, whether you are searching for a job, looking to improve or increase your current salary, thinking of starting a new business, or improving the fortunes of your current business. This spell should be performed during the time of a waxing moon.

You will need:

- A picture of the individual whose career you are attempting to improve
- One white candle
- Four green candles
- A small amount of basil oil
- Cinnamon incense
- A small amount of dried bay leaf
- Two green fluorite stones
- A few coins of various denominations
- A metal bowl
- A small white satchel

Instructions:

1.   At the center of what will be your sacred circle, arrange the four green candles in line with the cardinal directions. Place the white candle between you and the green candles. Place the incense to your left. Place the metal bowl to your right. Place the picture between you and the white candle.

2.   Cast the sacred circle.

3.   Put the bay leaf, the stones, the drops of basil oil, and
      the coins into the metal bowl. This will now be referred to
      as the "offering bowl".

4.   Center your energy.

5.   Light the green candle to the north, then the east, then
      the south, then the west.

6.   Lastly, light the white candle.

7.   Use the flame of the white candle to light the cinnamon
      incense.

8.   Wait a few seconds until the white candle produces some
      melted wax. Drip some of the wax onto the photo.

9.   Remaining focused on the photo, lift the offering bowl with
      your right hand and hold it at head height in front of you.

10.   While holding the bowl and focusing on the picture, recite
      the following:

"Success is coming soon to me.
Prosperity is flowing unto me.
So mote it be."

11.   Place the bowl back down in its original location.

12.   Visualize how professional success might manifest in your
      life and what it would look like. Imagine and visualize the
      route, the process it might take to reach you and make you
      more successful. The longer and more detailed you are able
      to hold this image in your mind, the more powerful your
      intent will be on the spiritual plane.

13.   Extinguish the green candle to the south, then the east,
      then the north, then the west.

14.   Lastly, extinguish the white candle.

15.   Close the sacred circle.

16.   Place the items from the offering bowl and the picture into
      the white satchel. Bury the satchel in the ground on the
      property where you live.

SPELL TO GET A DESIRED JOB

This spell is designed to bring you success in landing that perfect job... whatever that job is in your mind. This is your route to a financially and personally rewarding job or career.

This spell should be performed during a waxing moon. The symbol marked on the resumé should be something you specifically associate with the job you desire (like a badge shape for a police officer job, for example).

You will need:

- A small amount of Money Oil
- A small amount of saltwater
- A green candle
- A printed copy of your resumé
- An envelope
- A pen

Instructions:

1. Cast a sacred circle.

2. Light the green candle.

3.   Visualize your ideal job. Concentrate on the details (what are you wearing, what type of work environment is it, are there co-workers, how does your boss treat you, how much money do you make).

4.   Holding that image, wave your resumé through the smoke of the green candle. DO NOT ALLOW IT TO CATCH ON FIRE! This is called "censing".

5.   As you cense your resumé, recite the following: *"By air and fire, the job is mine."*

6.   Wet the corners of your resumé with the saltwater.

7.   While wetting your resumé, recite the following: *"By water and earth, the job is mine."*

8.   Dip your finger in the Money Oil and draw the symbol of your desired job on your resumé.

9.   As you anoint your resumé with the Money Oil, recite the following:

> *"The Sun does shine.*
> *The job is mine.*
> *The Moon does glow.*
> *To work I go."*

10. Fold the resumé and seal it in the envelope.

11. Address the envelope to: "Perfect Employer

Perfect Location"

12. Close the sacred circle.

13. Keep the sealed envelope in your sacred space for the next 30 days.

Spells for Protection

It is an unfortunate reality that, from time to time, we need to protect ourselves physically, emotionally, or spiritually. Just as there is light, beauty, and wonder in the world, there is also negativity, evil, and destruction. We can find ourselves purposefully targeted by other Wiccan or witchcraft practitioners who wish to do us harm or ensure that our magick does not produce results. These are types of black magick known as hexes and binding, respectively.

We can also find ourselves under attack from evil forces and entities which are not under the control of a human and have never walked through our plane in human form. I refer to these entities as "demons". Understanding that my choice of the word "demon" carries with it a certain amount of religious connotation, you are absolutely free to pick whatever word you wish for these bringers of darkness.

No matter the linguistic line you choose, we do need to know how to protect ourselves against them and their effects on our lives.

As modern Wiccans or practitioners of witchcraft, we enjoy a unique relationship with the spiritual plane. We purposefully open doorways between planes, alternate realities, and universal communication networks. No matter the intent we may have, it is important that we understand and accept the dangers we face as a result of our actions on the physical and spiritual planes. Despite our best attempts to remain spiritually safe, there is simply no way to ensure that the pathways we open will only be used by beings of light. So, what can we do to protect ourselves, our family, and our property from attachment by dark energy, negativity, and evil entities? Well, just like most needs, Wicca has some spells for that!

SPELL FOR PROTECTION FROM EVIL ENEMIES

You will need:
- A piece of paper
- A black pen
- A piece of black string
- Small amount of saltwater
- A freezer (if not performed in sub-freezing outside temps)

This spell is a type of binding to be performed when another Wiccan or witchcraft practitioner is using their magick to cause negativity in your life. The ritual is best performed during a new moon.

Instructions:

1.   Cast a sacred circle.

2.   On the piece of paper, write
the name of the person(s)
     affecting you.

3.   Tie a single knot in the middle
of the string. While tying
     the knot, focus on the negative
effects this individual has
     been causing in your life.

4.   Fold the paper up with the
piece of string tucked into the
     middle. Moisten the paper with
the saltwater (you do not
     want to soak it and obliterate
the name or names).

5.   Place the paper in the freezer
(or in a protected spot
     outside if performing the
spell in sub-freezing
     temperatures) and leave it
there until the situation has
     passed and the individual is
no longer affecting your life
     negatively.

THE WITCH'S BOTTLE

The Witch's Bottle is used to protect your home from negative energy and evil entities. Witch's bottles have been used for at least 400 years to protect the home by creating a magickal double of yourself. The supplies needed are a bit odd, but this is ancient magick after all.

The idea behind a Witch's Bottle is that the evil spirits are drawn to the bottle instead of you, and then get trapped by the nails, pins, and knotted string and confused by the broken glass/mirror (like a funhouse mirror maze).

You will need:
- A bottle with a tight cork or cap
- Nails and pins (preferably bent)
- Broken glass pieces and/or broken mirror pieces
- Pieces of string, knotted multiple times
- Your own nail, hair clippings, and bodily fluids (i.e., urine)
- A black candle (just to seal the bottle cap)

Instructions:

1.   Put   the   nails,   pins,   glass
pieces, mirror pieces, string,
       nail   clippings,   and   hair
clippings into the bottle. While
       adding the ingredients, recite
the following: *"Harm be
       bound away from me"*.

2.   Add the liquid ingredient.

3.   Close   the   bottle   and   seal   it
with the wax.

4.   Bury   the   bottle   upside   down
outside the front door of the
       home,   or   under   the
floorboards, or hidden in a remote
       corner of the lowest point of
your home.

SPELL FOR PROTECTION OF FRIENDS AND FAMILY

You will need:
- Salt
- Rosemary
- Angelica
- White Dandelion Fluff
- Small Crystal of Either Blue Lace
  Agate, Carnelian, or Garnet

- Slip of Paper with The Name of The Person to Protect
- White Sachet

Instructions:

1.   Cast a sacred circle.

2.   Place the salt, rosemary, angelica, dandelion fluff,
     crystal, and the slip of paper into the sachet.

3.   Focus on a visualization of the protected person. As you
     hold the visualization of this individual in your mind,
     recite the following:

     "I send you protection from all that may harm you. I send you the wish of safety. I send you the energies to keep you out of harm's way."

4.   Tie your sachet shut and gently kiss it focusing on your
     desires to send your friend or family member protection.

5.   Close the sacred circle.

6.   Place the sachet in a slightly open window to help send the

energies to the friend or
family member.

7.   Leave the sachet untouched for
a minimum of one hour.

8.   Following removal from the
window, the sachet can be
     emptied and cleaned for future
use.

SPELL FOR SPIRITUAL AND MENTAL PROTECTION

This ritual will allow you to create
an amulet for the purpose of
protecting yourself spiritually and
mentally from negativity and evil
forces. Wear or carry the amulet
whenever you feel the need for
spiritual and mental protection.
The amulet can be recharged from
time to time by using a new golden
candle.

You will need:
- A gold candle
- A pair of earplugs
- A flat stone, or piece of wood, or
  piece of metal (as amulet)
- Gold paint and a brush

Instructions:

1.   Cast a protective circle.

2.   Light the gold candle and recite the following: *"This
      is the power of silence."*

3.   Put in the earplugs.

4.   Concentrate on the power of spiritual and mental stillness
      as is found in the candle flame. When you feel calm and
      still, paint the bindrune on the amulet.

5.   Feel the power of the silent stillness flowing from the
      candle, through you, and into the amulet.

6.   Close the protective circle.

INCANTATION FOR PROTECTION OF BODY AND SPIRIT

This quick incantation and visualization allow you to protect yourself when an unexpected threat appears. Repeat the incantation a total of seven times. During each incantation, visualize an electric blue ring of flame encircling you

175

until you have a seven-ring spiral from head to toe.

Instructions:

1. Recite the following incantation (even if under your breath):

> *Power of the Goddess (or Goddess, Universe, Angels, Spirit,*
> *Ascended Masters, Protectors, etc.).*
> *Power of the God (or Goddess, Universe, Angels, Spirit,*
> *Ascended Masters, Protectors, etc.).*
> *Cool as a breeze.*
> *Warm as a stove.*
> *Flowing like a stream.*
> *Solid as a stone.*
> *So mote it be!*

CREATING A TALISMAN TO PROTECT LOVED ONES

There are times when what the world may see as a string of bad luck, we are able to recognize as signs of a negative or evil attachment to a loved one. Nothing makes you feel more helpless than when you *know* what is wrong with a spouse, close friend, or family member and yet they will not believe you or allow you to fix it. There is, however, a way that we can protect those whom we care about from being saddled with these attachments in the first place - a protective talisman. This is an object that they would carry with them most, if not all of the time which would act as a shield or hedge of protection around them and keep them safe from dark magick, negativity, and evil entities. Kind of like a good luck charm that works not by bringing good luck, but by keeping bad luck away.

You will need:

- 5 candles (1 yellow, 1 white, 1 green, 1 red, and 1 blue)
- A coin or object for each person you wish to protect
- Salt
- The juice from 1 lemon
- A small amount of ground clove
- A small black sachet
- An empty cup

Instructions:

1. Dress the five candles by rubbing them with lemon juice and ground clove.

2.   Place the coins or objects in the black sachet.

3.   Cast a sacred circle, using salt as the border.

4.   Draw a pentacle within the sacred circle using the salt,
     with each point touching the border.

5.   Place the yellow candle at the upper left point of the
     pentacle, the green candle at the lower-left point of the
     pentacle, the red candle at the lower-right point of the
     pentacle, the blue candle at the upper-right point of the
     pentacle, and the white candle at the top point of the
     pentacle.

6.   Place the black sachet and the empty cup in the middle of
     the pentacle.

7.   Because this spell draws heavily on elementals for
     protection, as you light each of the candles, say the name
     of the element represented. (Yellow for air, blue for

water, green for earth, red for
fire, and white for
spirit).

8. At the center of the pentacle,
take one of the coins or
objects from the sachet and
recite the following:

> *"Oh Goddess and God of all that
> is.*
> *Hear me and listen to my cry.*
> *Give protection to the person
> carrying this {coin or
> object}!*
> *Protect them with all your
> might.*
> *Let no evil befall them.*
> *Let no darkness cast its shadow
> upon them.*
> *So mote it be."*

9. Place the talisman into the
empty cup.

10. Repeat this process for as many
talismans as you are
creating, one at a time.

11. Allow the five candles to burn
themselves out.

12. Place the talismans back into
the satchel.

179

13. Close the sacred circle.

14. Take the remainder of the burned-out candles and bury them.

15. The talismans are now ready for you to give to those who
     they will protect.

SPELL TO BREAK A CURSE AND REVERSE THE EVIL

Although we try to protect ourselves from negativity, curses, and evil entities, there may be times when another follower of Wicca or witchcraft practitioner uses dark magic against us. Having a curse placed on you is a very dangerous situation to live through. As such, we need to be mindful that these instances do occur and that what may at first seem like a run-of-back luck may actually be something much more targeted and sinister.

The Wiccan Rede, and specifically the Rule of Three, can help us to break a curse that has been placed upon us and return the effects of the curse to the caster threefold.

You Will Need:

- A mirror
- A piece of paper
- A black pen
- A white candle
- A piece of white fabric

Instructions:

1.   Cast a protective circle.

2.   Light the white candle.

3.   Lay the mirror on the altar, reflection side up.

4.   Next, on the piece of paper, write all of the symptoms you are experiencing from the curse.

5.   Then, lay the paper upside down on the mirror and cover it all with the fabric.

6.   Recite the following:

> "*Your magick delivered*
> *A curse unto me.*
> *I remove and return*
> *Your curse back to thee.*"

7.   Press on the mirror through the fabric until it breaks (or
       smash it with a tool).

8.   Gather all of the pieces for disposal. Be careful not to
       either cut yourself on the shards, or see your reflection

       in any of the shards.

9.   Close the protective circle.

10.   You can either bury the mirror shards or dispose of them in
       your trash.

Love Spells

By far the most commonly performed type of spell is the love spell. Some spells can help you to open your heart to romance, while others can attract love to you.

There is a very clear distinction made within Wicca and witchcraft between "love" and "lust". There are spells for each, but it is quite important to be cognizant of which you truly desire. Love involves the possibility   of   a   lifelong commitment, to sharing the ups and downs of life, and establishing an emotional bond. Lust involves the quenching of carnal desires, the possibility of a very short-term relationship, and keeping the establishment of a physical bond. It is certainly possible for one to lead to the other, however when magick is used, it is more likely that you get what you ask for - no more, no less.

There is also one caveat that I would keep in mind when performing love spells. Take, for instance, a scenario wherein you perform a successful love spell aimed at a specific individual. That person does, in fact, develop strong feelings for you although they may not realize exactly why. What happens if it turns out that you are not able to reciprocate their feelings? What if you made an err in judgment and they are not the wonderful person you thought they were? What if they are unable to control their feelings for you when you lose interest in them, because the feelings are a result of magick? This scenario is not purely hypothetical. It has been played out before, to the detriment of the casting practitioner. You may have just magickly created your own stalker, or worse. I simply urge caution when performing love spells. It is fine and fulfilling to cast spells that open *your* heart or mind to love, or to attract souls with love to offer to you. But more often than not, danger lurks when one attempts to manipulate another unsuspecting individual into feelings or thoughts through the use of magick.

BASIC LOVE SPELL

This is a rather basic love spell designed to attract to you an individual who exemplifies the traits you desire in a love interest. After this spell is performed, keep your eyes open for new people joining your life or the development of new feelings for someone already present in your life.

This spell is best performed during a new moon when the stars are visible in the night sky.

You will need:

- 1 red candle with candle holder

- Rose petals
- Rose or lavender incense
- A rose quartz crystal
- 1 piece of paper
- A pen

Instructions:

1. Cast a sacred circle.

2. Light the red candle and place it on the altar.

3. Light the incense using the wick of the red candle

4. On the paper, write down all of the qualities that you are hoping for in a partner. Be as specific as possible. Try to envision the person, experience the feeling of being near them.

5. Read the list of qualities aloud. Then fold the paper and place it under the candle holder.

6. Take the rose petals and crystal into your hands. Look to the sky and find a star that appeals to you.

185

7.　　Hold your hands out, palms up, to expose the rose petals
　　　and the crystal to that star's light.

8.　　Recite the following:

　　　"The love *star, always burning bright,*
　　　Help and enable me in this spell tonight.
　　　Unify my true love with me,
　　　As I ask, so mote it be."

9.　　Sprinkle the rose petals around the base of the candle
　　　　holder.

10.　　Place the crystal in front of the candle holder.

11.　　Recite the following: "Hear me as I call to you. Come to
　　　　me, my love so true."

12.　　Allow the red candle to burn itself out.

13.　　Close the sacred circle.

LOVE KNOT

A love knot binds two people together so that they may come to realize they love each other and begin a romantic relationship. It is a very powerful spell and should be monitored, lest it leads to compulsion as described in the caveat above.

You will need:

- A length of silk string
- Pink chalk or salt
- 5 pink candles
- A small amount of ground cinnamon
- A small amount of Adam-And-Eve Plant root

Instructions:

1. Dress the 5 pink candles by rubbing them with the ground cinnamon and Adam-And-Eve Plant root.

2. Cast a sacred circle using either the pink chalk or salt to show the outer border.

3. Inside the sacred circle, draw a pentacle using either the

187

pink chalk or salt. The five points of the pentacle should touch the outer border of the sacred circle.

4.   Place one of the pink candles at each point of the pentacle.

5.   Light the pink candles beginning with the uppermost point and proceeding moonwise.

6.   Standing in the middle of the pentacle, take the piece of silk string and tie it into a knot.

7.   While tying the knot, recite the following: *"As I tie this knot, bring the love of {the name of the spell's target} to me!"*

8.   Repeat the tying of the knot and incantation a total of 6 times.

9.   When all 6 knots have been tied and the incantation has been said 6 times, burn the silk string in the flame of the uppermost pink candle of the pentacle.

10. All the pink candles need to burn themselves out.

11. Close the sacred circle.

12. Take the remnants of the pink candles and bury them in 5 separate holes.

LUST SPELL FOR INCREASED LIBIDO

There are times when love may not be what is missing. Married couples who have been together for a long time know exactly what I am talking about. Sometimes it can feel like your physical ship has sailed and you may struggle to find that red hot flame of passion that once burned so bright inside. If you would like to reignite your libido, this spell should put you directly on the path to a smile-filled, reinvigorating, evening with your partner.

This is a spell that is to be performed during a sunny day, as it draws upon the power of the God (sun). Best results will be seen by performing this spell on a Friday.

189

You will need:

- A red candle with a candle holder
- A food or drink thought of as an aphrodisiac (for example, hot peppers, whiskey, ginger candies, cherries, or olives)
- A small amount of patchouli oil

Instructions:

1. Dress your red candle by rubbing it with the patchouli oil.

2. Take your dressed candle and your aphrodisiac of choice outside into the sunlight. Pick a spot where you can sit, meditate, and not be disturbed.

3. Light the red candle.

4. Gaze into the flame of the candle and allow yourself to be consumed by the moment. Imagine the fire coming into you and filling you with its heat. Feel it explicitly enflaming your groin and arousing your natural carnal instincts.

5.   As you concentrate on this sensation, recite the following:
        "I am fire. I am heat."

6.   Eat or drink your aphrodisiac. Feel the heat of it as goes
        into your body. Let your skin tingle. Let the experience
        radiate into your entire body.

7.   As you concentrate on this sensation, recite the following:
        "I am fire. I am heat."

8.   Extinguish the red candle. Take it home with you and place
        the candle near your bed.

9.   At the earliest possible convenience, have sex with your
        partner   in   the   bed. Throughout,   refer   to   the
    visualization
        of the fire being a part of your body, of keeping the flame
        alive within you. Allow the heat to be a part of you at
        your very core.

CREATING A FIRST DATE CHARM

Is there anything more exciting AND terrifying as a first date? The jitters, the hope of a blossoming relationship, the fears of will you like them and will they like you! There is a way to stay calm and enjoy those feelings without becoming overwhelmed by them. A first date charm. It may not guarantee that this person will be your one true love, but at least it will keep you relaxed long enough to find out for sure.

The blue paper in this charm ritual is meant to represent calm and to help keep your head clear. The red ink is here to encourage an open heart to receive romance.

You will need:

- A piece of blue paper
- A pen with red ink
- A pair of scissors

Instructions:

1. Visualize your intention clearly - a relaxed, happy date going well. Picture laughter and ease. Nothing forced or disingenuous. Just feel a glow of peace and hope for the future.

2.   While   holding   this
visualization, write the first name
of
     your date on the paper.

3.   Draw a circle around the name.
Carefully cut the paper
     along the circle.

4.   Fold the paper into thirds.
While folding, recite the
     following:

     *"With this I have
     the eyes to see.
     True love or not,
     So mote it be."*

5.   Place the folded paper in your
shoe during the date.

As a testament to this charm's
efficacy, I used this exact ritual
prior to going on the first date
with the person who became my
partner, my one true love. This
year, we celebrated our 20th wedding
anniversary.

BRINGING LOVERS TOGETHER

Here is an example of a decidedly
modern spell meant to solve a modern

problem. In the age of internet dating, it is more possible than ever before to fall in love with someone far away from your location - from a different city to halfway around the world. But that does not have to mean that you are destined for a solitary life with short bursts of happiness achieved through Zoom or FaceTime.

This is a spell designed to bring long-distance lovers together. The point of this spell is to already be in a loving and committed relationship, but living far apart, with the intent of either cohabitation or at least living in much closer proximity. Spread out over 10 consecutive nights, this spell should be performed during a waning moon.

You will need:

- A small amount of saltwater
- Lavender incense
- A map, showing where each of you live (a printout or something you create yourself would be fine)
- Scissors and tape
- A pen

194

Instructions:

1.   After lighting the incense,
consecrate the map by anointing
      each corner with saltwater.
Then pass the map through the
      smoke of the incense.

2.   On the map, mark each of your
locations with a hand-drawn
      star.

3.   Cut the map in two, closer to
the star representing where
      you live.

4.   Cut away a strip of the
distance between you.

5.   Tape the map back together. As
you do, recite as follows:
      "We   are   coming   closer
together. So mote it be."

6.   Repeat steps 4 and 5 each night
for 10 consecutive nights.

7.   On the 10th night, cut away all
the remaining distance.
      When you tape it together, the
stars should touch each
      other. On that night, recite
the following: "We are

together. So mote it be."

8.   Fold the map so that the stars are on the inside.

9.   Take the map outside and burn it. The ashes that scatter to the breeze fly to your joint destiny. If you are unable to burn the map outside, burn it safely indoors and scatter the ashes to the breeze later.

RITUAL BLESSING OF ROMANCE

If you are already in the romantic relationship you have always wanted, but wish to have it blessed, there is a beautiful ritual you can perform. This ritual is meant to stabilize a romance desired by both parties. It is not intended to be, nor should it ever be used, as a one-sided spell.

For best results, carry out this ritual on a Saturday night during a waxing moon.

You will need:

- 2 glass beads (one the color of your birthstone and one the color of your partner's birthstone).
- At least 1 foot of brown thread.
- A small amount of saltwater
- Incense (preferably something earthy, like patchouli or lemongrass)

Instructions:

1.   Cast a sacred circle.

2.   Light the incense.

3.   Pass the bead representing you through the incense smoke and then dip it into the saltwater.

4.   Recite the following: *"By air and fire. By water and earth.*
This is me in relation to {the name of your partner}."

5.   Pass the bead representing your partner through the incense smoke and then dip it into the saltwater.

6.   Recite the following: *"By air and fire. By water and earth. This is {the name of your partner} in relation to me."*

7. Pass the thread through the incense smoke and recite the following: *"Air binds our minds to earth. Fire binds our passion to earth."*

8. Dip the thread in the saltwater and recite the following: *"Water binds our hearts to earth. Earth binds us together."*

9. Thread the two beads together on the string and tie the string together using 7 knots.

10. With the tying of each knot, recite the following: *"With the power of seven, we are blessed. Blessed be."*

11. Take the amulet outside and bury it.

SPELL FOR NEW LOVE

This spell is designed to bring love into your life by focusing on attracting a loving energy.

For best results, perform this spell on a Friday night during a waxing moon.

You will need:
- 7 pink candles
- 7 red candles
- Incense (Rose or Valerian)
- A list of 9 attributes that your dream partner would possess (Available for love, live in my state, athletic... for example)

Instructions:

1.   Set up the 14 candles in a heart shape surrounding you.
     They should be arranged alternating pink, then red, then pink, then red...

2.   As you light each pink candle, recite the following: "I light for love".

3.   As you light each red candle, recite the following: "I light for passion".

4.   Once all 14 of the candles have been lit, read your list aloud, preceding each trait with a plea to the Goddess in the form of "Goddess send me...".
Just as an example, perhaps

you would say, "Goddess send me a woman who wants to have children".

5.   This list is your prayer, treat it as such. Channel all of your mental and spiritual energy into this prayer. Continue to send your energy into the universe until the candles burn themselves out. As they begin to extinguish themselves, close the prayer with *"So mote it be."*

Spells for Health and Healing

The majority of work that a white witch does is in the arena of health and healing. The person being helped can be yourself, a loved one, or a client and the type of healing can be physical, mental, emotional, or spiritual. As you can imagine, with this many options, the permutations of spells and rituals which can be performed is quite vast. Finding the correct spell for the correct individual to heal the correct problem at the correct time is not simple. It is, however, extremely rewarding; and an excellent way to use the powers you are developing magickly as well as psychically.

Let me take a moment to make one thing very clear. The use of spell work to physically heal the body is NOT meant to be a substitute for modern medical treatment. Your work on the spiritual plane can, and will, have tremendous effects on physical illness; however, it should be seen as a companion to treatment from a medical professional. The two should work hand in hand with each other to heal a physical ailment. What modern medicine views as "miraculous" only appears that way to those unaware that much magickal work may have gone into securing that result.

Let's start by taking a look at some ways to address and heal emotional trauma, both in ourselves and in others.

RITUAL FOR A POSITIVE ATTITUDE

It can be downright amazing just how mean we can be to ourselves. Beyond just the old adage of "I'm my own worst critic", some of us face negative thoughts about ourselves which actually make us "Our own worst enemy". Many of us find it easier to forgive others for their own shortcomings than to forgive ourselves for the same.

I was in this pattern of negativity myself at one point in my life, living in an unending loop of "I am a loser and so I do not deserve love, yet if I had love I would be less of a loser." However, what I came to realize was that this line of thinking ignored all of the positive aspects that made me a unique and wonderful soul. That negative line of thinking was a self-fulfilling prophecy whispered into my ear from a very young age by darkness and deceit, by an unseen enemy in order to convince me of my worthlessness. Darkness, evil, the devil - whatever you wish to call it - whispers to us all at one point or another in our lives. It is up to us individually to decide whether we will listen or not.

One way of breaking free of negative thoughts and a negative attitude towards ourselves is by performing this ritual. It is a very simple undertaking and, as such, you will get out of it what you put into it.

Take your time in creating the lists and try to search your subconscious mind to gain these insights. We are all beautiful balls of positive energy contained in a meat-suit on this plain. Try not to get distracted by the meat-suit and focus on the light within.

There is no specific day of the week on which to perform this ritual. For the best results, I suggest performing the ritual during a waxing moon.

You will need:

- A sheet of paper
- A pen
- A pair of scissors
- A white candle
- A metal bowl or cauldron

Instructions:

1. Prior to beginning any magickal or cleansing rituals (including a ritual bath), draw a line down the center of the sheet of paper. In the column on the left, write all of the negative things you have thought or heard about

yourself. Be specific, honest, and don't hold back. This is your opportunity to purge yourself of all of the negativity which has been holding you back.

2. After writing the negative side of the list, follow-through and complete any pre-ritual cleansing that is planned.

3. Cast a sacred circle.

4. On the right side of the divided paper, write a list of all of your positive attributes; all of the positive things you have thought or heard about yourself. Again, be honest and specific. The only rule is that you must have at least as many positives as you do negatives written down.

5. Light the white candle.

6. Cut the paper down the centerline, separating the positive list from the negative list.

7. Using the flame of the white candle, light the negative

list on fire and place it in
the metal bowl or cauldron to
burn.

8.   As the negative list burns,
read aloud the positive list.
Take your time and focus on
each attribute. Read each as
follows: "I   am   _____.
Blessed Be. I am _____.
Blessed Be…"

9.   After   reading   the   final
attribute, end the ritual with "So
mote it be."

10. Allow the white candle to burn
itself out.

11. Close the sacred circle.

12. Keep the positive list with you
and read a few of the
positive attributes any time
that negativity attempts to
re-enter your mind and steal
your light.

ANTI-NIGHTMARE MOJO BAG

A "mojo bag" is a common technique
employed in magick. It is a small
sachet bag, which is filled with
many different items depending upon

the spell. The mojo bag might then either be kept with the practitioner or buried to act as a barrier.

If you have been plagued by nightmares, you know the negative effects that the disruption to your sleep schedule, and the terrifying images that accompany the nightmares, can have on your daily life and your health. Nightmares can be a sign of an evil attachment, a signal that you are being attacked psychically through black magick, or the purging of violence and fear by your own subconscious. No matter the cause, being awoken several times per night by nightmares can lead to devastating impacts on your physical and mental well-being. For the self-care aspect of avoiding consistent nightmares, this mojo bag is being included in the "Health and Healing" section.

One of the steps in this preparation is to anoint your "third eye" with water. The "third eye" is the pineal gland located inside the brain. However, we can approximate the third eye with a spot located about one inch above where our eyebrows would meet. This is the spot to anoint in this spell.

You will need:

- A small white or blue sachet
- A piece of silver ribbon
- A silver marker or paint pen
- Cedar shavings or cedar chips
- A piece of charcoal (for censing the cedar shavings)
- A small amount of saltwater
- Anise seeds, rosemary, and thyme

Instructions:

1. Cast a sacred circle.

2. Draw a crescent moon on the outside of the sachet with the silver marker or paint pen.

3. Light the charcoal and place the cedar shavings or chips on top.

4. When the cedar begins to smoke, cense yourself with the cedar. As you cense yourself, recite the following: "*I bless my dreams by the power of air and the power of fire.*"

5. Cense the sachet through the cedar smoke.

207

6. Anoint your third eye with the saltwater. As you anoint,
recite the following: *"I bless my dreams by the power of
water."*

7. Splash a small amount of saltwater onto the sachet.

8. Point your athame at the mixture of anise seeds, rosemary,
and thyme. Direct your energy through the athame and into
the herbs. As you direct your energy, recite the following:
"I bless my dreams by the power of earth. So mote it be."

9. Place the herbs into the sachet and tie it closed with the
silver ribbon.

10. Close the sacred circle.

11. Sleep with the mojo bag under your pillow to vanquish your
nightmares and enjoy a good night of sleep.

ELEMENTAL HEALING - WATER

The four natural elements are extremely important in healing spells. Each element has specific healing qualities ascribed to it and ways to efficiently direct those qualities. Although each of the following elemental healing spells are written in self-healing language, they can easily be converted to heal others either locally or remotely.

Water is considered the gentle element of healers. The fact that our bodies consist mostly of water may explain why water is so strongly associated with healing across a wide range of ailments. Physically, water is used to heal diseases of the blood and lymphatic symptoms. It is also the element used to assist in pregnancy issues. Psychologically, water is used to help with symptoms of depression, mood swings, and sleep disorders.

The drinking of wine within a sacred circle is also a way to specifically incorporate the element of water into your magick.

You will need:

- Fresh, clean water in a goblet
- Rose incense

Instructions:

1.   Cast a sacred circle.

2.   Holding the goblet of water, describe your intention and
       invoke the power of the element of water to aid in your
       healing.

3.   Speak to the water in the goblet. Gather the energy from
       around and within you and focus it into the water. Touch
       the water, allow yourself to feel absorbed by the element.

4.   Pour the water over yourself. Be sure to get water on any
       specific parts of your body which need healing.

5.   Focus and "feel" the water soaking and incorporating itself
       into you, feel the power of the element changing and
       healing you from the inside.

6.   End the spell by reciting the following: *"So mote it be."*

7.   Close the sacred circle.

ELEMENTAL HEALING - AIR

The element of air is used in the physical healing of ailments of the lungs, which makes sense. When it comes to the more emotional side of healing, the element of air is used to provide a clear mind, to call upon inspiration, and to encourage logical thought patterns.

One often overlooked aspect of the healing power of air is the representation of the element through speech. The use of the spoken word is, after all, a manipulation of the air. As such, healing of ailments or the calming of fears related to speech or public speaking can be addressed through the element of air.

Because air is constantly present all around us (hopefully) at all times, we do tend to become desensitized to its presence. A daily routine of meditation and mindfulness can help us to pay more attention to the air around us. However, in the meantime, or if you are not interested in developing this type of daily routine, the use of a hand fan can bring the air to the forefront of our consciousness.

You will need:

- A hand fan
- Incense associated with the element of air (i.e., lavender, sage, lemongrass, meadowsweet, etc.)

Instructions:

1. Cast a sacred circle.

2. Announce your intention and invoke the power of the element of air to aid in your healing, by reciting as follows: *"I invoke the power of the air, the element of the body, and of the mind, to heal the suffering being caused by the {ailment}."*

3. Light the incense. Breathe deeply. Gather the energy from around and within you, as the air you take in becomes a part of you.

4. As you feel the air dissipate within you, recite the following: *"Air, power of creation and destruction, I bring you in."*

5.   Fan the incense smoke over yourself, from head to toe.

6.   End the spell by reciting the following: *"So mote it be."*

7.   Close the sacred circle.

ELEMENTAL HEALING - FIRE

The element of fire is associated with healing neurological and autoimmune disorders, issues with libido and a failing spiritual energy. It is useful for raising your life force. When doing spell or healing work using the element of fire, bring as much energy into the sacred circle as you can muster. It is also helpful to add the crystals of amber or tiger's eye, extra candles, and incense representative of fire such as basil or rosemary.

There are instances when calling on the element of fire can be detrimental to the healing process, even if the list of symptoms calls for this type of healing. Because fire *is* energy (both physically and spiritually speaking), and is extremely powerful, some

213

individuals may be too weak or in too delicate a state to treat with the fire element immediately. In these instances, it is recommended that the first round of healing be performed through the element of water in order to bolster and prepare the energy and spirit of the individual seeking the healing.

You will need:

- A grouping of 9 red candles bound together using orange ribbon

Instructions:

1. Cast a sacred circle.

2. Light the grouping of red candles.

3. Gaze into the flames of the grouping. Much like when using fire for divination, allow your eyes to lose focus and allow your consciousness to melt into the flame.

4. Bring the fire close to you mentally and physically. Recite the following: *"I invoke the power and energy of healing fire."*

5.   Hold the candle grouping near the portion of the body which
        needs healing. If an emotional healing is being requested,
        hold the candle grouping near the third eye.

6.   Focus on the heat and move the feeling of that heat
        throughout your body. Allow the heat to fill your entire
        body and being until you can imagine being lit, aglow, from
        the inside.

7.   As you feel the warmth envelop and begin healing you,
        recite the following: *"Fire, heal me."* Repeat this
        incantation 9 times.

8.   End the spell by reciting the following: *"So mote it be."*

9.   Close the sacred circle.

ELEMENTAL HEALING - EARTH

The element of earth rules the physical body (or your "meat suit", as I have called it). As such, it is vital in the healing of muscle, bone, tissue, and organs. Earth is also associated with appetite and eating disorders, both anorexia and morbid obesity.

Emotionally, earth is a stabilizing, strengthening, and grounding element. It roots us in the here and now, in the current moment, which can be very helpful in the treatment of Post-Traumatic Stress Disorder.

You can bring additional earth elements into your spell work by including salt, the consumption of bread, milk, limestone, granite, and organic potting soil or organic gardening soil.

You will need:

- Limestone or granite rocks (enough to surround your workspace within the sacred circle
- A brown candle
- A small amount of Mugwort
- A small amount of olive oil
- A small amount of salt
- A small bowl of organic potting soil

Instructions:

1. Dress the brown candle by rubbing it with the olive oil and
rolling the candle in crushed Mugwort.

2. Cast a sacred circle.

3. Use the limestone or granite rocks to create a small circle
around what will be your healing workspace.

4. Light the brown candle.

5. Announce your intention and invoke the power of the element
of earth to aid in your healing, by reciting as follows: "*I
invoke the power of the earth, the grounding root of my
physical form. Earth! Heal me! Earth! Heal me! Earth! Heal
me!*"

6. End the spell by reciting the following: "*So mote it be.*"

7. Allow the brown candle to burn itself out and bury the
remnants.

8. Close the sacred circle.

SPELL FOR LONG-DISTANCE HEALING

There may be times when we need to heal someone who is too far away for us to lay our hands on. This spell will work for a wide variety of different types of healing. It can be modified to fit the ailment(s) from which your client or loved one is suffering, or even combined with elemental healing if so desired.

The sacred circle that is cast at the beginning of a spell work session or ritual serves a number of protective purposes. However, it also serves as the gateway between our plane and the spiritual plane. On the spiritual plane, distance does not exist in the same way it does on the physical plane. It is this property of the spiritual plane which allows for healings, spells, astral projections, etc. to take place over what would be excessive distance here on the physical plane.

This spell includes a slight modification in the casting of your sacred circle in order to highlight the "black hole" style property. In step one, when you have finished

218

your regular casting of the sacred circle, recite the following:

> *"This is a circle between worlds, sacred, protected, a source of power and a gateway of manifestation. Here all things are possible. This is a location without location, existing in two planes and in all places at once. So mote it be."*

You will need:

- A photograph of the person being healed
- A personal item of the person being healed (this can be a snip of their hair, a button from their clothing, etc.)
- Incense of frankincense & myrrh
- A small amount of saltwater
- A small amount of mint oil

Instructions:

1.   Dress the white candle with the mint oil.

2.   Cast a sacred circle using the modified language from
     above.

3.   Light the incense.

4.   Cense the photo and personal
item through the incense smoke
        and recite as follows: *"By air
and fire, this is {Name of*
        person to be healed}. {Name}
is here in this circle. This
        is {Name} and {Name} is here!"

5.   Wet   the   photograph   and
personal item with saltwater and
        recite as follows: *"By water
and earth, this is {Name}.*
        {Name} is here in this circle.
This is {Name} and {Name} is
        here!"

6.   Lift the photo and personal
item towards the Goddess and
        God and recite as follows:
"Lady and Lord, see that this is
        {Name}. See that {Name} is
here. Beloved Goddess and God,
        lend your aid as I heal {Name}
in this circle. So mote it
        be!"

7.   Focus all of your energy and
stare at the photograph of the
        person to be healed. Repeat the
phrase, *"You are healed"* as

you send the healing energy to the individual. You can
        repeat this phrase for as long as you can maintain your
        focus on the photo.

8.   Close the sacred circle.

9.   Keep the photograph and the personal item in a safe and
        secure place.

Healing Salve

This is a witchy salve that is something I keep on hand at all times. It is handy for a large range of small wounds and pains – cuts, bruises, dry skin, chapped lips, headaches, insect bites, and bee stings.

You will need to infuse extra virgin olive oil with the herbs and flowers listed prior to making the salve. To infuse the oil, place the herbs and flowers in a large glass jar; pour the olive oil into the jar, keep the jar in a sunlit window, flip the jar every day for 30 days. After 30 days, strain out the herbs and flowers using cheesecloth and discard them. The oil is what you will be keeping for use in the preparation of the salve.

This salve is very protective and healing. It also contains properties of travel magick, so it is perfect for taking on vacation!

You will need:

- Equal parts of Comfrey Leaf, Calendula Flowers, Plantain, and St. Johns's Wort
- 1 cup of extra virgin olive oil
- 1 piece of cheesecloth (for straining)
- A chunk of beeswax (approximately 1 once)
- A small amount of lavender essential oil
- A small amount of tea tree essential oil
- A small amount of Vitamin E oil

Instructions:

1. Infuse the extra virgin olive oil with the herbs and
    flowers as explained above.

2. Melt the beeswax over low heat. Be sure not to burn it,
    just melt it.

3.   Once the beeswax has melted, pour in your infused olive oil. Let the mixture warm up while stirring with a wooden spoon until it is fully combined.

4.   Take the pan off the heat and add 6 or 7 drops of lavender essential oil, 6 or 7 drops of tea tree oil, and 6 or 7 drops of Vitamin E oil. Give the mixture a quick stir.

5.   Pour your salve into small glass jars or aluminum tins and let it harden. The salve will remain antiseptic and safe for use for up to a year (although with small children, I usually run low in about 6 months).

Candle Spell for Quick Healing

This is a classic-style candle healing spell. The goal of the spell is to aid in lessening the effects of an illness and speeding up recovery.

The size of the candle you choose should reflect the severity of the illness and length of recovery time you are manifesting. A votive or a small taper candle may be enough for a short-term illness, while a more serious malady may require a large seven-day candle for instance.

You will need:

- A white candle
- A small amount of healing salve
- A small amount of dried motherwort
- A glass candle holder appropriate for the candle chosen

Instructions:

1.   Dress the white candle with the healing salve and dried
        motherwort.

2.   Place the dressed candle in the candle holder.

3.   Light   the   candle   for   5-10 minutes per day in the room with
        the individual who needs to be healed. Upon lighting the candle,
        and **each** time you light the candle, recite the following:
        "*The Lady and Lord shall watch over you and grant you the*

gifts of health and comfort. So mote it be."

4. Day by day, burn the candle until either the candle no longer lights (in which case, repeat the spell), or until the individual is fully healed and recovered.

5. When the spell is complete, dispose of the remains of the candle in the trash to rid the afflicted and the home of the illness for good.

Third Eye Opening - Psychic Spells

Remember the section on Psychic Abilities and Divination? Well, this is where the proverbial rubber meets the road. The "Third Eye" is the name ascribed to the portion of our brain which sees the unseeable. The third eye is a part of us which only some choose to acknowledge and develop. The third eye is the key to our psychic abilities. However, although often described only in esoteric terms, the third eye does go by another much more familiar biological name - the pineal gland.

The pineal gland was the last inter-cranial gland to be discovered. In 1640, Renee Descartes identified and named the gland nestled deep in the center of the brain, referring to it as the "seat of the soul". However, it would take another 318 years before an American dermatologist, Aaron Lerner, in 1958, discovered that the pineal gland exclusively produced a molecule he dubbed "melatonin".

The pineal gland is a tiny, pine-cone-shaped organ seated on the bridge between the right and left hemispheres of the brain. It is located approximately 1/2 inch above the center point between your eyes and straight back to the center of your brain.

What does any of this have to do with the third eye? Well, the pineal gland (located *inside* the center of our brain and in no way connected to the optic nerve which feeds signals from our eyes) is photosensitive! Melatonin is the molecule that regulates our circadian rhythm (making us tired at night and awake during the day). So somehow, the pineal gland releases melatonin when there is a lack of sunlight even though it is not linked to the optic nerve. That's right. The pineal gland is very literally a "Third Eye" and is located exactly where the third eye chakra has been depicted since the time of the ancient Sumerians!

The belief that the pineal gland is just the modern term for the rediscovered third eye organ known about for centuries past just shows how much wisdom has been lost and regained throughout the ages. Perhaps Descartes was exactly on point with his "seat of the soul" description.

There are ways for us to open our third eye and begin to develop our abilities to access the spiritual plane, including a meditation routine, the use of some herbs and plants, and of course through the use of spells and rituals.

Part of the journey of practicing Wicca or witchcraft is to open yourself to your psychic abilities. The more open you are, the better you will be able to communicate with

the energies around you and the more
power your intentions will hold.

You will need:

- A small amount of as many of the
  following dried herbs as
  possible: Mugwort, acacia,
  honeysuckle, peppermint,
  rosemary, thyme, cloves, yarrow,
  dandelion, lilac, lavender, and
  calendula
- A purple sachet
- A silver marker or paint pen
- A silver candle

Instructions:

1. Cast a sacred circle.

2. Using the silver marker or
paint pen, draw an eye on the
    purple sachet.

3. Place the herbs into the
sachet.

4. Light the silver candle. As you
light the candle, recite as
    follows:

    "*I open my eye, for the better
    to see.*

May these herbs awaken me.
By the power of 3 times 3,
My third eye open. So mote it
be!"

5.   Touch the sachet to your third
eye.

6.   Repeat the incantation, touch
the sachet to your third
       eye, twice more.

7.   Allow the candles to burn
themselves out.

8.   Close the sacred circle.

9.   Store the sachet under your bed
or beneath your pillow.

There are herbs and essential oils
which can assist you in the opening
and clarifying of your third eye and
psychic abilities. These herbs and
oils should be respected. Some may
be safely topically applied, some
may be safely ingested, and some are
only safe in aromatic form. It is,
as always, important to speak with
a reputable herbalist to know
exactly how safe an herb or oil may
be for topical use or ingestion.

- Angelica Root
- Cypress
- Elemi
- Frankincense
- Helichrysum
- Juniper
- Marjoram
- Patchouli
- Rosemary
- Sandalwood
- Vetiver

There are also a number of crystals that can aid us in our attempts to open and clarify our third eye and psychic abilities. For our purposes, placing a crystal or a few crystals on a table at our bedside can help to open our third eye as we sleep. Also, placing some of these crystals on your body, including one crystal in the center of your forehead over your third eye, during meditation can open your psychic center.

- Amethyst
- Angelite
- Axinite
- Azurite Sun
- Blue Aventurine

- Blue Tourmaline
- Celestite
- Chiastolite
- Dumortierite
- Fluorite
- Labradorite
- Lapis Lazuli
- Moonstone
- Phenacite
- Pietersite
- Purple Sapphire
- Purple Tourmaline
- Rhodonite
- Shungite
- Sodalite
- Sugilite
- Quartz

Please understand that when you open your third eye, you are opening a link between your spirit and other dimensions, other planes of existence. As you begin to open your third eye, you will experience some visions and other physical effects. Imagine having been blind since birth and then beginning to see for the first time ever. How confusing, strange, and frightening the sensation of vision would initially be! That is exactly what you ARE doing. You could begin to sense shadows or see other-worldly beings. Remain calm and rest assured that what you are sensing is real and is natural. You are not causing the sensations, you are just now able to see what has always been around you. Stretch your atrophied psychic muscles and begin to develop your abilities.

Personal Power Spells

If there was one word to summarize the draw, the feeling, of practicing Wicca and performing witchcraft it would be: EMPOWERMENT. Witchcraft allows an individual to perform magick, on the spiritual plane, in direct contact with all of the ancient wisdom contained in the universe, without the need of an intermediary priest or other religious leader. Witchcraft is about our power to function on separate planes. Witchcraft is a display of our power.

To be able to display our powers, it is necessary for us to be able to enhance our power, to gather our power from around us in order to direct it into our spell work.

Spells to enhance and gather our personal power can be as individualized as we are. There really is no wrong way to empower yourself, as long as you are respectful and do so without ill intent. So, you can feel free to use these spells as a framework for your own spells or rites, but they do not need to be strictly followed.

You will need:

- A quartz crystal
- A black tourmaline crystal
- A white candle
- A bundle of dried sage
- A cauldron or metal bowl

Instructions:

1.   Cast a sacred circle.

2.   Place the black tourmaline crystal in front of you.

3.   Light the white candle. Use the flame of the candle to
     light the sage bundle.

4.   Once the sage is smoking, place it in the cauldron or metal
     bowl.

5.   Pick up the quartz crystal and cense it using the sage.

6.   While holding the quartz, close your physical eyes and open
     your third eye. Visualize energy being gathered from all
     around you, swirling into you through your third eye.
     Energy flows up from the ground and into you. Visualize
     your aura growing stronger and brighter with each wave of
     energy that enters you.

7.   Recite the following: "*I am magickal. I am powerful. I am
     compassionate. I am loved. I am strong.*"

8.   Repeat the affirmation 6 additional times.

9.   As you begin to feel more and more powerful, as you feel
     magick surging through you, recite the following: "*Magick
     running through me, help me see with clarity. Power that I*

have summoned here, protect me and I will have no fear."

10. Repeat the incantation 6 additional times.

11. When ready, end the spell with "*So mote it be.*"

12. Quench the white candle and close the sacred circle.

SPELL TO PERPETUATE ENERGY AND POWER

This spell is best performed during a new moon. As the moon's light increases night by night, so will your gathering energy and power.

You will need:

- A small amount of bay leaf essential oil
- A small amount of frankincense essential oil
- A small amount of jasmine essential oil
- A small amount of eucalyptus essential oil

- 1 yellow candle in a candle holder
- 1 red candle in a candle holder
- 1 blue candle in a candle holder
- 1 green candle in a candle holder

Instructions:

1.   Dress the yellow candle with bay leaf essential oil.

2.   Dress the red candle with the frankincense essential oil.

3.   Dress the blue candle with the jasmine essential oil.

4.   Dress the green candle with the eucalyptus essential oil.

5.   Cast a sacred circle.

6.   At the center of the circle, place the yellow candle to the North, the red candle to the east, the blue candle to the South, and the green candle to the west. You will be standing in the center of this secondary circle.

7.   Light the candles in moonwise order, beginning with the yellow candle.

8.   Recite the following: *"I enter the flow of all that is. I*
     am   filled   with   loving-kindness. I release all negative and
     unbalanced   energies.   And   I draw the best of power to me. So
     mote it be."

9.   Relax   and   center   yourself. Visualize a continuous flow of
     energy passing from each of the four candles and entering
     into you through your feet and emanating up into your body.
     Feel the unlimited power fill you.

10.   When you feel that you have been filled with as much power
     as   you   are   able   to   take, visualize the energy flow
     stopping.

11.   Extinguish   the   candles   in counter-moonwise order.

12.   Close the sacred circle.

13.   With a clean cloth, wipe the remainder of the candles.
     Carry the cloth with you and, whenever you feel your powers

begin to falter, smell the cloth for a quick recharge.

Cleansing Rituals

Being a practitioner of Wicca and witchcraft means that we are opening ourselves to the spirit world. As a result, we enjoy the ability to use our magickal power to affect change on the physical plane. However, it also means that we are accessible to a wide range of negative and/or evil entities. These entities exist for no reason other than to cause pain, distress, confusion, and havoc. And, as witches, we are seen as prime real estate for these destructive energies. These negative entities also find their way to unprepared and unsuspecting individuals. These individuals then become affected, oppressed, or even possessed by these evil entities. Unless, of course, they find their way to us first and we are able to cleanse them of their attachments. The removal of negative or evil entities from a space or an attached individual is called "cleansing".

Performing cleansing rituals is a vital task in sweeping away bits of negativity and darkness that may be present in a space or attached to an individual after breaking a curse or any type of psychic attack. Picture it this way, you had been shackled to darkness, chained to evil. When you break or explode from a chain, there are tiny bits or shards of metal that go flying off. They may be too tiny to see with your eyes, but if you walk around in bare feet you are guaranteed to end up with a sliver. Breaking a curse or a psychic attack tends to leave behind tiny shards of that negativity and evil. If you allow it to remain in your space, your soul is guaranteed to end up with a sliver. When you get free - stay free.

There are many thought processes and beliefs surrounding cleansing rituals. Every religion from Catholicism to Hinduism to Rosicrucianism has their "own". However, the truth is that, when viewed as a whole, they share more similarities than differences. As a result, there is really no harm to be done by trying one, two, or even all of the ritual examples which follow. All are designed to do the same thing: rid the space (and thus the people within the space) of negative energy and ward against the re-emergence of evil. So, explore. Find what works best for you, your space, and your lifestyle.

Unlike the majority of tasks in the spiritual realm, a successful cleansing will result in **immediate** relief. Oftentimes, although not always, when there is a negative presence or evil remnants are left from the breaking of a curse or spell, a general feeling of heaviness or unease will pervade a space. The stronger the negativity, the stronger the feeling. When you are able to rid your space of the negativity, the feeling of unease and the heavy atmosphere will disappear along with it. You will know that it worked because you will feel that it worked.

It is extremely important to continue cleansing until all of the evil and negativity has been removed. An evil or negative entity can be further enraged and empowered by a half-hearted attempt at cleansing it. The cleansing rituals quite literally hurt and weaken the entity. If the cleansing is not carried through, the entity will resume its prior actions with a much greater resolve and a newfound revenge-filled rage. Remember, we are making things better, not worse.

1.   **Smudging**

Smudging is probably the most widely accepted and practiced cleansing ritual. Smudging is the burning and smoldering of herbs wherein the smoke is used as the cleansing agent. The most commonly used herb for smudging is a bundle of sage, specifically white sage. Sage is the kryptonite of dark entities (whether they be demons or restless spirits). However, a variety of different herbs have actually proven equally effective, including basil, lavender, and clove.

I personally use a mixture of dried herbs consisting of Mugwort, white sage, and lavender when performing a smudging session. I have found that Mugwort works as an excellent boost to my psychic abilities during the smudging session, allowing me to better sense the presence of the negativity or evil; while the sage and lavender work together to rid the space of the offending entities.

The "ritual" is actually extremely simple. It is one of the few rituals to preferably be performed during the daylight hours.

A smudging session should begin with a prayer or call for protection for anyone who will be in the home during the session. Next, the aura and body of each person present for the session should be cleansed. This is done by lighting the herb bundle and, once it is smoldering, tracing the outline of the person with the bundle, allowing the smoke to rid the aura and individual of any attachments they may be carrying.

Be sure to have at least one window or door open on each floor of the home. The negativity must be given a way to escape or it will be trapped and further enflamed.

Next, the smudging bundle should be carried into each corner of each room and public space in the home. Carry something to catch any of the smudge bundle ashes that may drop off (I use an abalone shell). Do not forget closets, basements, attics, side rooms, enclosed porches, etc. Once each and every space has been cleansed, you have finished the ritual.

There really are not any specific words that <u>must</u> be said during a smudging session. It is really up to those present to use visualization to help the smoke guide the negativity out of the home. However, some tend to give a short incantation within each room. If you choose to speak, commit to it being in each space and keep it simple. Perhaps something like, *"In the name of the Lady and the Lord, I implore all negativity and evil to leave this space. You have no right here and shall hold no power here."* or *"Through the power of the Spirit, no negativity or evil shall remain in this home."*

Smudging is not even a ritual that should be used only to cleanse from a brush with evil. I smudge myself and my aura once every two weeks, and my home 3-4 times per year. It is a great way to maintain a clean aura and stay free of unguided attachments by evil entities, and to keep my home clear of pockets of negativity.

2.   Salting

Salting is a widespread practice in eastern cultures, but it is quickly becoming accepted by the west as well. Salt has long been known as a purifier. Like quartz, salt's crystalline structure has the ability to hold and trap negative energies. It is a passive way of cleansing your environment of darkness.

There are a few different ways of deploying salt as a cleansing agent.

- A bowl of salt beside the front door (perhaps on a foyer table) can be used to attract and trap negativity or evil from individuals entering your home.
- Salt can be sprinkled in the corners of rooms in order to draw the negativity. Be sure not to touch the salt while it is deployed as a cleanser. After 4-5 days, vacuum or sweep up the salt and dispose of it.
- Salt can be used to encircle the outside of a home as a protective measure against the invasion of evil.
- Lastly, salt can be added to bathwater to create a cleansing

soak for the individual working with the spirit realm.

It is important to note that I am not referring to common table salt. Table salt has been processed with iodine. Iodine affects the structure and clarity of the salt crystals. You will want to use whole or shaved pieces of unrefined sea salt or unrefined mineral salt. Don't worry, it is not as difficult to find as it sounds! A simple Google search will bring up many inexpensive suppliers.

3.   Incense

The use of incense began, as far as we can tell, with the Egyptians who used it in healing rituals and the Babylonians who relied upon it when conferring with their divine oracles. The use of incense arrives in Japan in the sixth century - where it was used in purification rituals for the emperor and his court.

Today, incense can be found in a large number of scents and forms. Not to mention incense holders ranging from simple to amazingly intricate.

Incense is best used for personal and small area cleansing. Much like smudging, the smoke is the cleansing agent. However, unlike smudging, incense remains situated in one room. Just light the tip, blow out the flame and place the incense in the holder.

Among the best incense to burn for a cleansing ritual are:

- Sage
- Sandalwood
- Lavender
- Frankincense
- Palo Santo
- Linden Flower
- Juniper
- Hibiscus

4. Tuning Fork

Sound and music have been used in healing rituals for thousands of years. Early civilizations used singing bowls for sound therapy and Greek physicians used instruments and vibration to treat sickness and combat insomnia. Using a tuning fork for cleansing is merely an extension of the same idea. Tuning forks vibrate at specific frequencies. The frequency of 417 Hz is known as a "Solfeggio frequency" and has been found to rid the body, mind, and physical space of negative energy. It is not an absolute "must", but a fork tuned to the frequency of 417 Hz would undoubtedly be the most useful.

Find a comfortable spot within each room of your home. Set your intention for a cleared, renewed space. Lightly tap the tuning fork against something solid. Close your eyes and let the sound vibrate around and through you, allow it to clean all of the negativity and evil out of the room and you. Move on to the next room and repeat the process.

Unhexing, Banishing, and Eradicating Curses

The powers of evil and personal destruction that accompany a curse or a hex can be extremely strong and grow like a cancer, embedding themselves deep in our lives and psyche. It may, and most likely will, take more than one spell to free ourselves from this type of darkness.

This is not a one-and-done situation. I visualize curses and the other types of psychic attacks much like a mangrove tree. What appears on the surface to be a large swath of mangrove trees of many acres, or even an entire swamp, can actually be only one large mangrove tree. As the roots of a mangrove grow, they spread in all directions, not just down into the earth, and produce periodic shoots back above the surface. These become what appear to be separate and distinct trees, but are actually part of the original root system.

So it is with curses and darkness in our lives. What might appear to be unconnected traits or instances of negativity may, in fact, all be fed by the same curse. Just as you would not expect to kill a 4-acre wide mangrove system by chopping down one of the trees on the surface, we cannot expect to break a widespread curse or hex which has pervaded many aspects of our lives by performing one spell one time and then moving on.

That is why we need to see the fight against darkness as an ongoing war and not just a single battle. We need to be willing to fight for ourselves, our destiny, and for our bloodline. It may take repeating the same incantation once per day, or once per week, over an extended period of time to finally dig out the last effects of a curse in our lives. It may take performing the same ritual on successive new moons for a number of months to break a strong hex. It may even take a combination of the two! But please know that we are on the side of good, of light, of love, and of righteousness. We WILL prevail.

When you should utilize these prayers is completely up to you and your needs. A witch's link to the spiritual plane is always available. That is the beautiful thing about incantations, they take very little preparation and there is never a bad time to perform them. It is important to focus and calm your spirit, open your heart and mind. When you perform an incantation, whether inside or outside of a sacred circle, put your all into it.

Spell work is normally performed at night, under the light of the moon.

Unless otherwise noted within the spell, it is safe to assume that the spells and rituals are meant to be performed at the time of the waxing moon. Also, there is a specific way to maximize the power you are putting out into the universe - try to perform your ritual near running water (i.e., a creek, a river, an underground spring, etc.). The electromagnetic energy created by running water is a natural, measurable fact. It is electromagnetic energy that powers our intentions into the universe and into the spiritual plane. Therefore, if you are able to be near a source of electromagnetic energy, your intention will gain strength merely by being in the location. As you are preparing yourself for the ritual, focus your intention and calm your spirit, cast your sacred circle, and make your intentions known clearly.

SPELL TO BREAK A MULTI-GENERATIONAL CURSE

It is an extremely important portion of this spell work that you be as cleansed as possible prior to performing this ritual. You should bathe in saltwater, cleanse your energetic aura with incense, focus your intention and calm your mind.

This spell should be performed on the night of a full moon.

What you will need:

- A small sachet or locket-style necklace
- Sea or Mineral Salt
- Coriander (Cilantro)
- A small drop of your blood (to be harvested during ritual)
- A black candle
- A Selenite crystal

Instructions:

1. Cast your protective circle.

2. Light the black candle. Use the flame to calm your spirit
    and set your intention - you will be undoing powerful dark
    magic that is transferred through generations.

3. When you feel focused, place a small amount (a pinch) of
    the sea salt into the sachet or locket.

4. Harvest the small drop of blood and put the blood onto the
      salt.

5. Add the coriander (cilantro).

6. Pick up the Selenite crystal. Slowly moving the crystal
      above the sachet or locket, recite the following:

> *"A darkness has followed*
> *in the blood of rich and poor.*
> *I purify with salt and fire*
> *to be accursed nevermore."*

7. Add one drop of the wax from the candle.

8. Tie the bag closed or close the locket.

9. Close the sacred circle.

10. Keep this sachet or necklace on your person every day until
      the next full moon. At that time, you may decide whether to
      dispose of the sachet/locket or to keep it.

It is most assuredly odd to include blood into a white magick spell. The reason blood is included in this spell is due to the type of curse (multi-generational). The power of the curse and the negativity is transferred and travels through the bloodline from generation to generation. Therefore, the only way to break the curse is to cleanse the blood of the curse. That is done through the purifying salt and the Selenite crystal. The cilantro is meant to contain the curse within the sachet or locket. There are times when the necessity of using bodily fluids in white magick does come up, but as you read other spellbooks or Books of Shadows, be aware that most uses of blood or bodily fluids are linked to the dark uses of black magick.

SPELL TO BREAK A CURSE AND REVERSE THE EVIL

Sometimes just breaking a curse is not enough and doesn't give you closure on the attack. Instead, we aim to break the curse and send the negativity back to the cursing witch. When you have been attacked spiritually by another witch or Wiccan practitioner, you are absolutely justified in returning whatever was released upon you.

You Will Need:

- A mirror
- A piece of paper
- A black pen
- A white candle
- A piece of white fabric

Instructions:

1.   Cast a sacred circle.

2.   Light the white candle.

3.   Lay the mirror on the altar, reflection side up.

4.   On the piece of paper, write all of the symptoms you are experiencing from the curse.

5.   Lay the paper upside down on the mirror and cover it all with the fabric.

6.   Recite the following:

"Your magick delivered
A curse unto me.
I remove and return
Your curse back to thee."

7.   Press on the mirror through the
fabric until it breaks (or
      smash it with a tool).

8.   Gather all of the pieces of the
mirror for disposal. Be
      careful   not   to   either   cut
yourself on the shards, or see
      your reflection in any of the
shards.

9.   Close the sacred circle.

10.   The   mirror   shards   can   be
disposed of simply in the trash.

BREAK A CURSE USING A TALISMAN

With this ritual, you will create a
talisman to absorb the negative
energy of a curse and then destroy
it, taking the negativity with it.
This spell should be performed
during a new moon.

You will need:

- Air drying clay
- Water charged with sun's energy
  (solar water)
- A slip of paper and pen
- Bay leaf

- Black candle
- Cauldron or metal bowl
- Toothpick

Instructions:

1. Cast a sacred circle.

2. Sprinkle some of the solar water within the circle and on yourself.

3. Light the black candle.

4. Write down on the slip of paper all of the effects that the curse has had on you (be thorough and specific).

5. Fold the paper around the bay leaf. Set the bundle on fire and place in the cauldron or metal bowl.

6. When the ashes are finished smoldering, set them aside.

7. Take a portion of clay and anoint it with a drop of solar water. Mix the ashes into the clay thoroughly. Roll the clay into a ball and then flatten it into a disk shape.

8.   On one side of the disk, use the toothpick to inscribe a
     symbol to represent the curse (it can either be a sigil or
     just a simple doodle that represents the curse to YOU).

9.   Close your sacred circle.

10. Extinguish the black candle and allow the talisman to dry.

11. Once the talisman is dry, allow it to sit and charge in the
     sun.

12. Carry the talisman with you constantly to allow it to
     absorb the energy from the curse.

13. On the next new moon, take the talisman and smash it,
     rendering the curse that the talisman has absorbed broken.

14. Dispose of the shards outside of your home. Be sure that no
     residue of the talisman remains in your home or on your
     person.

QUICK INCANTATION FOR PROTECTION OF BODY AND SPIRIT

This quick incantation and visualization allow you to protect yourself when an unexpected threat appears. The greatest way to stay safe during a curse or hex is to not be hexed or cursed in the first place! So this incantation and visualization is a wonderful way to protect yourself from even being in a negative situation.

Instructions:

1. Recite the following incantation (even if under your breath):

"Power of the Goddess (or Goddess, Universe, Angels, Spirit, Ascended Masters, Protectors, etc.).

Power of the God (or Goddess, Universe, Angels, Spirit, Ascended Masters, Protectors, etc.).

Cool as a breeze.
Warm as a stove.
Flowing like a stream.
Solid as a stone.
So mote it be!"

2.   Repeat the incantation a total
of seven times.

3.   During   each   incantation,
visualize an electric blue ring of
     flame encircling you until you
have a seven-ring spiral
     from head to toe.

THE WITCH'S BOTTLE

Witch bottles have been used for at
least 400 years to protect the home
and its inhabitants from curses,
hexes, and evil by creating a
magickal double of yourself. The
supplies needed are a bit odd, but
this is ancient magick after all.

The idea behind a Witch's Bottle is
that the evil spirits are drawn to
the bottle instead of you, and then
get trapped by the nails, pins, and
knotted string and confused by the
broken   glass/mirror   (like   a
funhouse mirror maze).

You will need:

- A glass bottle with a tight cork
  or cap
- Nails and pins (preferably bent)

- Broken glass pieces and/or broken mirror pieces
- Pieces of string, knotted multiple times
- Your own nail, hair clippings, and bodily fluids (i.e., urine)
- A red or black candle (just to seal the bottle cap)

Instructions:

1.   Put all solid materials into the bottle while reciting the following: *"Harm be bound away from me"*.

2.   Add the liquid ingredient(s). Close the bottle and seal with the wax.

3.   Bury the bottle upside down outside the front door of the home, or under the floorboards, or hidden in a remote corner of the lowest point of your home.

CREATING A JAMAICAN DUPPIE BAG

A "duppie" is the Jamaican term for an evil spirit or ghost. This sachet functions in a very similar way as the more familiar "mojo bag", however the Jamaican Duppie Bag is specifically geared toward ceremonial magick for protection and the banishing of freshly evoked evil spirits.

There is an ingredient in this preparation which you may not be familiar with - asafoetida. Asafoetida is an herb produced in Southern Iran, used in Indian cuisine, and integral to the Jamaican Duppie Bag. How is that for a multi-cultural plant! But don't panic because it can be found in most grocery stores and online in many forms.

You will need:

- A black sachet
- A black ribbon
- Asafoetida
- Camphor
- Garlic

Instructions:

1. As you fill the sachet with the asafetida, camphor, and garlic, recite the following: *"My Lady and Lord, of both*

moonlight and sun. See me safe, free of evil. Cause the darkness to run. So mote it be."

2.   Tie the sachet closed with the ribbon.

3.   Carry the Duppie Bag with you whenever you feel you may need protection from darkness or evil.

As an aside, I personally keep my Duppie Bag hanging from the rearview mirror of my vehicle so I can put it in my pocket at any time. We just never know when evil may try to gain a foothold.

SPELL TO BANISH EVIL AND NEGATIVITY

This is a simple ritual to banish harmful influences from your home and the bodies within. The red apple is seen as a symbol of purity, beauty, and rebirth in the Wiccan pantheon. This ritual should be performed on a Friday during a waning moon.

You will need:

- 1 red apple

- 1 bay leaf (this should be a fresh leaf)
- A piece of red string

Instructions:

1. Cast a sacred circle.

2. Place the apple in front of you.

3. Take a moment to focus your intent. Focus your mind on
    sending away all negativity and evil.

4. Visualize a protective layer around you, like the skin of
    the apple, which makes all negative energies bounce off.
    Keep this image firmly in mind.

5. Use your athame to cut the apple vertically into two
    halves. Lay the halves in front of you cut sides up.

6. Place the bay leaf on one of the cut halves.

7. Recite the following: *"With red and green, I form a
    banishing dome. Cast all evil from within my home."*

8.   Repeat   the   incantation   two
additional times, finishing with
     "So mote it be."

9.   Put   the   two   halves   of   apple
back together (leaving the bay
     leaf   inside)   and   secure   them
with the red string.

10.   Close the sacred circle.

11.   Bury   the   apple   on   your
property, the closer to your home
     the better.

UNCROSSING RITUAL

An "uncrossing" means to get rid of
unwanted and unneeded energies and
attachments   that   may   have   found
their way or been thrust upon you.
Perhaps you are suffering from a
hex-related illness or you feel as
if you have unintentionally been
saddled with an oppressive negative
entity, an uncrossing ritual may be
exactly what you need to heal or
free yourself.

You will need:

- 7 Bay Leaves (fresh or dried)
- 2 sticks of frankincense incense

- A small amount of ground cinnamon
- 1 white candle
- 1 plate (not made of plastic or paper)

Instructions:

1. Cast a sacred circle.

2. Light the white candle.

3. Place the Bay Leaves on the plate.

4. Sprinkle the ground cinnamon onto the bay leaves. While you do this, recite as follows:

> *"In the name of the great and victorious elements, I invoke the ancient forces. To crush and remove all negative entities, all curses and crosses. Break and dissolve. Bless and set free. As it is now, so mote it be."*

5. Cross the two sticks of incense on the plate over the bay leaves and cinnamon. Light them.

6.   Allow the white candle and the incense to burn themselves out.

7.   Close the sacred circle.

8.   Any remains of the incense sticks, bay leaves, cinnamon,
    and the white candle can be disposed of in your trash. They
    do not need to be buried.

BULLY BANISHMENT JAR

As much as we hate to admit it, bullying and mean-spirited behavior is as much a part of the adult working world as it was when we were in school. Young, unconfident, spiteful children often grow up to becoming older, unconfident, spiteful adults. They may be in our personal lives in the form of neighbors or in our professional lives in the form of coworkers, but the realities are the same. Nobody likes a bully. We may not be able to banish these individuals from our lives, however we can banish the negative effects that their words and actions have on us. With a little help from a pickle jar. You won't need to cast a sacred circle at all for this ritual and it is

266

perfect for your kitchen right at home!

You will need:

- A glass jar with a screw-type lid (I use pickle jars)
- 1/4 cup of apple cider vinegar
- A small amount of dried mint

Instructions:

1. Take the jar into your hands. Visualize the individual doing you no harm and simply leaving you in peace. Hold this image in your mind.

2. Recite the following: "*{Person's name}, you will bully and intimidate me no more.*"

3. Add the vinegar to the jar.

4. Add the dried mint to the jar.

5. Screw the lid tightly onto the jar and shake vigorously as you recite the following 9 times: "*Venom, viciousness, and vileness be gone!*"

6.   Open   the   lid   and   pour   the
contents down the drain under hot
      running tap water. Visualize
all of the mean-spirited,
      vile,   nasty   remarks   and
behavior of the bully being washed
      down the drain and out of your
life.

7.   Rinse the inside of the jar and
recite as follows:
      "*{Person's   name},   your   power
over me is gone. I am safe*
      *from   harm.   I   am   no   longer
troubled by you and I am free. No*
      *more   will   you   distress   me.   I
am stronger than you. So mote*
      it be."

8.   Dispose   of   the   jar   in   the
trash. You wouldn't want any of
      the energy from that jar being
carried over into the next
      spell or use for the jar.

CHAPTER 4 - MAINTENANCE & DISCLAIMER FOR PROFESSIONAL ASSISTANCE

How to Know if Your Magick is Working

Once we have done all of our research, gathered ingredients, and performed our spell or ritual, how do we know if what we have done is having any type of effect on the physical plane? How are we to monitor whether the power and effort we pour into our magick is having the desired manifestations? It seems like it would be so simple. In our modern world, we have become accustomed to easily drawing conclusions between cause and effect, to understanding how "Action A" will change the state of matter around us. However, just like the majority of magickal practices, the spiritual plane does not function under the same

269

rules as our day-to-day, physical plane.

That means that we need to be looking, and feeling, in different ways to monitor our spell efficacy. So, let's jump in and take a look at a few of the ways we can tell if our magick is working.

1.   *Signs from The Universe*

As Wiccans or practitioners of witchcraft, we need to be cognizant and mindful of signs and signals from the Universe at all times. However, perhaps no time is more important than following the casting of a spell or performance of a ritual. The Universe is constantly sending us all kinds of signals, but we need to be ready to receive them. Signs can come in the form of weather changes, cloud formations, actions of wildlife, or many other types of seemingly "natural" occurrences.

2.   *Mood Changes*

Perhaps some of the most common signs that any spell is

working is how the spell caster is feeling. A successful spell should lead to a feeling of happiness, of clarity, of satisfaction, and of confidence. When you have given your all to a spell or ritual, when you believe in your personal power and your magick, you *should* believe that what you have done will result in the manifestation you have desired. Often, we notice this change as an instinctive feeling in our surroundings. We simply "feel" that our spell is working, we just "know" that our magick is making the required change to our world. Your subconscious will certainly make you aware if you have been true to yourself and true to the Universe, either through manipulation of your mood or through manipulation of your dreams.

3.   *Messages in Dreams*
Dreams are not just random images as your brain runs a "de-frag" program. All of our dreams have meaning. Being

able to interpret that meaning can be very enriching and can allow us to receive signals from our subconscious which will help us to know if a spell is working.

4.   *"Coincidences"*

I put coincidences in quotes because I truly do not believe that coincidences exist. What many see as a coincidence is actually a signal from the Universe. We need to be open to seeing signs in coincidences, even if the message is not immediately clear or understandable.

Have you ever found yourself thinking about a friend or family member you haven't spoken with in quite some time, only to have that person contact you within the next few hours? The world would consider that a coincidence. However, we may recognize this moment as a signal from the Universe. The message being relayed is for the practicing witch to decipher, as only he or she can be aware of all of the intricacies, feelings, and spell work performed.

Further, it is important to remember that the spiritual plane does not function on your time, which is a good reason to avoid spell work that has a hard deadline. Even if a spell is completed perfectly and with enough power the first time it is performed, just because you want to see the completed manifestation within the first week, there is no guarantee that the Universe will comply with your timeline. In the same vein, just because you do not see the completed manifestation within the first week, does not necessarily mean that the spell was not successful.

We work on a plane outside of the known laws of physics, including those governing space and time. We are able to take advantage of this fact during some of our spiritual activities, like astral projection. But the seeming disregard to timing can be a rather frustrating difference with which to come to terms. Practitioners of witchcraft need to be patient, watch for signals and remain open to receiving confirmation of efficacy through non-traditional channels and not necessarily on cue.

Where Do You Go From Here?

Great job on getting this far! Now you have learned how to craft and cast spells on a wide array of subjects. And, best of all, you have trained your mind and discovered how to identify and develop your innate power to manifest effects on the physical plane. So you may be wondering, "Now what? Is this it? I am officially a witch, so I guess I just wait until I need something." No! You are just now beginning to scratch the surface of Wicca, of witchcraft, and of the spiritual journey that you have embarked upon. So, let's discuss taking the next steps!

First and foremost, LEARN! The world of magick is vast and deep. No matter how much you know, read, and learn, there will always be something new to explore, something new to learn. Perhaps you have already found a spiritual and magickal path that resonates with you. Perhaps you are still searching for your place in the universe. Either way, you should familiarize yourself with as many different schools of magick (and as many different schools of thought) as you possibly can. Each have something special to offer you. Each can lead you to new personal discoveries. And one of the exciting facets of witchcraft is that you are free to mix-n-match! Find the ideas, the spells, the theories, etc. that make sense and resonate with you and incorporate them into your own practice.

Learn about tangential fields of study like astrology, numerology, feng shui, tarot, demonology, etc. All of these ancient subjects have something to lend you and your spell work or may open doors into fascinating additional studies and expand your understanding of yourself and the world around you.

I am going to make a confession that you will not see from many authors: I do not know everything about any subject. That is why there is a "Resources" page at the end of this book. Yikes. But I have no fear in making that statement because the dirty little secret is that **nobody** knows everything about any subject! There is no shame in admitting that there is more to learn. Never run from knowledge.

Secondly, you need to PRACTICE! Any athlete or musician will tell you that in order to develop their talent they had to commit to an enormous amount of practice. And those same athletes or musicians will also tell you that to maintain and improve their talent they have committed to an unending cycle of practicing. Magick is simply not a spectator sport. You will never become a powerful, comfortable practitioner of Wicca or witchcraft by just reading about it. The more spells and rituals you perform, the easier they will become and the more confident you will become in your own ability.

So, meditate regularly, practice sensing energy, perform spells, try alternate forms of spells, practice working with various components, pay attention to your dreams, and keep a journal. These are all important factors to incorporate into practice. Do not give up on your magick. Your power is in there, it is a part of you. Putting your knowledge into practice is how you can release it. Just keep going.

Third, maintain a deep connection with NATURE. Try disconnecting from our technologically-laden world for long periods. Developing a rapport with the natural world will serve you in three ways: the majority of the ingredients used in spell work can be found in the natural world (herbs, flowers, stones, and crystals), you will give yourself an opportunity to become more in tune with the cycles of the earth, and nothing nourishes the soul more than time spent with Mother Earth. A happy witch is a naturally balanced witch.

Fourth and finally, consider practicing with OTHER PEOPLE. If you have been practicing your craft solo, consider looking around your area for like-minded individuals with which to practice some of your spell work. Yoga centers, health food co-ops, and

New Age or occult supply stores can all be good places to start asking around. There are advantages and disadvantages to practicing with other individuals. It is something to consider, but not something I would necessarily recommend everyone try. It really just comes down to a matter of personal preference. Some advantages can be:

-    It can be fun to share ideas and spend time with
         "kindred spirits";

-    You can learn a lot from other people's experiences
         and perspectives; and

-    Combining your energy with someone else's can ramp up
         the power of a spell significantly.

However, there are also disadvantages to consider, such as:

-    If your energies or intentions are not compatible
         with those of the others in a group, your spells can
         get confused and murky;

-       If you are working with
people who tend to be
            domineering, or if you
are insecure about your own
            abilities, you can end
up being unduly influenced by
            another witch. No matter
how long they have been
            practicing,   and   no
matter how powerful they profess
            to be, they are just
human like you. Never allow
            anyone to control your
magick or to make you do
            anything with which you
do not 100% agree.

Spiritual Activities
Requiring Professional
Assistance

I cannot possibly be the only one
to have had this happen. You are
driving down the highway when your
vehicle decides to make some sort
of   horrific   sound,   kind   of   a
whining and simultaneous grinding
sound. Immediately you pull over
to the shoulder and pop the hood.
You find yourself staring under
the hood of your vehicle, pretty

much just hoping that whatever is wrong would start to glow or you would find something completely obvious that would get you back up and running. But, alas, you are doing little more than perusing your engine compartment and silently nodding to yourself like, "Yep. The engine is still there." Do you know what we needed in that situation? Help from a professional! And there is nothing wrong with that!

What can be even more dangerous is when we are staring at ourselves or a loved one in a spiritual crisis while we nod to ourselves like, "Yep. Gonna need to fix this on my own because I do not want anyone else to know about it." That is the kind of thought pattern that has pervaded far too much of society today. There is no need to save face when it comes to crises of the soul. They are a condition of being human and literally every human goes through them at some point. Just as we have been speaking and discovering ways over the previous chapters and sections to manifest our desires and manipulate spiritual energies on alternate planes of existence, we must also take into consideration that sometimes our knowledge is not enough, and it is time to garner the help of a professional.

We can, and should, feel empowered to explore our own spirituality at our own speed and in our own time. However, there are specific situations when we require more than our own power and knowledge. Some of those instances are:

1. Yoga

Yoga is far more than just a set of stretching exercises. Actually, yoga is a group of physical, mental, and spiritual disciplines originating in India over 5,000 years ago. It is based on an extremely subtle blend of art and science focusing on healthy living.

The word "Yoga" comes from the Sanskrit word for "to unite". Yogic scriptures state that the aim of the practice is to unite the individual consciousness with the Universal Consciousness, harmony between mind and body, between man and nature. This state is known as "nirvana".

The practice of Yoga involves training of both the body and the spirit. Make no mistake, Yoga is a spiritual practice… a religion… with its own set of scriptures (The Vedas) and its own leadership (gurus and yogis).

Although it can be difficult today to find even a small town in America without a Yoga studio or a Namaste t-shirt, it is important to remember that respecting the religious beliefs of others is a foundation of Wicca and witchcraft. The physical aspect of Yoga is a wonderful workout and is something that can be learned online or by many other methods. If you want to join a Yoga group in the park, try hot Yoga, or see what the big deal is with goat Yoga - go right ahead and have fun.

However, the spiritual side of Yoga is extremely complex. When it comes to learning the beliefs associated with Yoga and the union of humans and nature, I recommend seeking the assistance and the teachings of a professional yogi or guru.

2.   Demonology

As a practitioner of white magick, we turn ourselves into targets, willingly. Over years of practice and study, an example of how a negative spirit experiences a white witch has become more and more clear.

Picture yourself in complete darkness, the type of inky blackness that does not allow you to see your own hand in front of your face. Nothing to see, nothing to feel, no way of orienting yourself in space (are you facing up or down), no way of being sure whether your eyes are even open or closed... for hundreds of years. The only thoughts in your head are of anger, panic and confusion. And then, suddenly, there appears a tiny ball of light. Your mind rushes to decipher whether the light is close but tiny, or large but far away. Since you can block the tiny light with your hand, it must be off in the distance. You rush toward it. As the light begins to grow in size and clarity, you realize for the first time in far too long that you are not alone in the darkness. You can suddenly sense other beings around you, seemingly drawn toward the same light as you. Some feel as though they have been there longer, some feel as though they are relatively new, and others feel like nothing you can put into such a category. These "others" do not even feel like people to you. They have no human energy, they have no residual spirit, they have no memories that they are giving off. More or less, you experience them in waves of hatred and repulsion. And the "others" are far faster than you, making you feel small and insignificant. You get the distinct impression for the first time in your existence that you are in the presence of a predator and that you are prey. These are demons. They are drawn toward the glow of the presence of light in the darkness, just like every other malevolent spirit, except they are well aware of what they are chasing. They want the white witch. They want to extinguish the light and exist in the darkness. Their only reason for being is to cause harm, pain, distress, fear, destruction, and death to all creatures of light.

There is no need to believe in the concept of a "heaven" or "hell" to believe in demons. Frame the idea in whatever context you wish, but the reality stays the same. There are entities that exist both in our physical plane and on the spiritual plane that consist purely of evil. I refer to these entities as "demons", although that is merely a label that I use because it is one with which I am comfortable and accustomed. You can feel free to use any word you desire.

Demons are evil entities, not spirits, who have never walked the earth as a human. They were never born in a meat suit, lived a life, died, and had their energy released back into the Universe. They have always existed in the form of negativity and are able to pass through dimensional planes only when a portal is opened from our side. Witches open such a portal any time they cast a sacred circle, the link to the spiritual plane, although their space is protected by the properly cast circle. However, there are many other unsuspecting individuals opening portals who are completely unprotected; and even leaving the portals open between dimensions allowing for free travel of spirits and demons alike.

One way of "accidentally" inviting a demonic entity is by the use of a spirit board (or Ouija Board). When an individual opens themselves to be entered and manipulated by the spirit of their dead grandfather, there is absolutely no way of guaranteeing that is the spirit that responds… if it is a spirit at all. This complete lack of control is why I never agree to the use of a spirit board, regardless of the skill level of the individual or witch involved.

Another manner of coming into contact with the demonic is through black magick. As we have discussed, white magick is used for good and pure manifestations only. Any magickal spell that injures, causes pain, causes misfortune, causes sickness, or causes harm to another is considered "black magick". The use of black magick should be strictly avoided for two reasons. First, the Wiccan Rede (which we discussed earlier) states:

> *"Bide the Wiccan law ye must, in perfect love and perfect trust.*
> *Eight words the Wiccan Rede fulfill: If ye harm none, do what ye will.*
>
> *What ye send forth comes back to thee, so ever mind the Rule of Three.*
> *Follow this with mind and heart,*
> *Merry ye meet and merry ye part."*

In other words, any black magick you perform, the universe will return to you three-fold. Not good folks. Not good. Black magick relies on the demonic to fulfill the desires of the witch. Witches who practice black magick do not worship demons or "the devil", however they do call upon demons (often by name) to assist them in their curses, hexes, and other dark rituals.

Demons are extremely malicious, destructive, ancient, and intelligent. There is a huge difference between the ability of a white witch (new or experienced) being able to banish negative energy, banish a negative spirit, clear a chakra, or bless a home and banish a demon from a residence or, worse yet, from an individual. Yes. I am referring to exorcism, though by another name. "Exorcism" is a Catholic ritual. "Banishment" is a spiritual boot in the ass of evil without the trappings of Catholicism.

Banishing or exorcising a demon is not a practice that should be undertaken by a single witch, regardless of their skill level. When we encounter the demonic, it is time to seek professional, specialized, help.

Where the help comes from is a matter of personal choice. It can be a Catholic priest, a non-denominational Christian priest, a Shaman, a Reiki Master, a practitioner of black magick may even be able to help, or a seasoned coven of white witches. Just DO NOT ATTEMPT TO BANISH A DEMON BY YOURSELF. Demonic attachment, oppression, and possession are a reality even in our technologically driven, shiny, plastic world.

3. Modern Medicine

Please let me make this very clear. Nothing within the belief system of Wicca, nor the practice of witchcraft, precludes or even dissuades one from seeking assistance from a medical professional. To be frank, modern medical practice and the practice of witchcraft work quite well hand-in-hand, although you would be hard-pressed to find a doctor to admit such. Modern medicine is, at its most basic, a re-introduction of age-old herbal remedies. The majority of today's wonder drugs are rooted in known herbal and pharmacological processes and properties. Today's doctors would have been persecuted as witches in previous centuries. They may call their healing "science" and we call our healing "magick", but truthfully, we are not using knowledge that is all that different.

So when we are sick, when we are in pain, or when we experience a physically traumatic event, we treat ourselves AND we seek professional help.

The same concept relied upon in the medical field above also applies to the psychological field. There have been psychological issues that I have been able to discover through meditation and self-reflection, come to terms with, and overcome without the need for any external assistance. But there have also been instances wherein I needed help with an emotional issue and have sought out assistance from a trained professional. Psychologists and psychiatrists use tactics not unlike those found in guided meditation to reach the root of an emotional issue. There is no shame in asking for help when delving into a place in our own minds which has been locked away for our protection. Sometimes the issue is simply too painful or deeply guarded for us to reach on our own. Find a professional to help guide you safely to your realization.

CONCLUSION

Congratulations! You have taken a huge step toward becoming a knowledgeable, practicing witch and/or Wiccan! Hopefully, you feel informed and empowered to work on the spiritual plane and to see your desires manifested in your life.

This is the comprehensive, vetted, and plain-language reference guide that all beginning witches and practitioners of Wicca have longed for. Within these pages, you have a reference guide for all of the basics you need to be a successful white witch or practicing Wiccan. We have discussed:

- The history of witchcraft;
- The basic principles, beliefs, and practices of Wicca;
- The yearly Sabbats and Wiccan calendar;
- The different types of magic and witchcraft;
- Do's and Don'ts of witchcraft;
- Psychic Abilities
- Divination

- Grounding and drawing your energy
- Ritual preparation
- Creating an altar and a safe space for your practice
- The basic tools you will need (your toolkit)
- Herbs and their uses
- Crystals and their uses
- Candles and their uses
- Over 45 basic spells
- Signs and signals that your magick is working
- The next steps on your journey
- Instances when you should seek professional assistance

I would love to be able to boil all of this information down into a tidy little sentence that you can simply carry off with you as you begin your practice. But, as we discussed, witchcraft is a lifelong journey of learning and exploring. Any bite-sized soundbite I could offer would never encapsulate the powerful and truly amazing spiritual enlightenment which Wicca and witchcraft offer each of us.

If I can leave you with one parting thought, let it be this: The Universe is infinitely more vast and remarkable than we could ever possibly grasp while tethered to our meat suits. There are planes of existence within planes of existence. And yet something about being human allows us an all-access pass to the wonder. Something about being human draws our consciousness towards the heavens and out into the vast unknown. Something about being human allows us to be one with nature and in control of nature simultaneously. Perhaps there is something unique about being human within the Universe and its dimensions. Perhaps we are all somehow part of a much greater whole. Perhaps miracles are not random at all. Perhaps it is all magick.

Do not fail to venture out into the Universe, my fellow witches. This is our workspace. If ye harm none, do what ye will. Walk ahead as witches. Walk ahead in confidence. Walk ahead not in fear, but with respect.

THANK YOU

I would like to end this by saying
a huge thank you for taking the time
to learn from myself. I really hope
this book gave you exactly what you
were looking for and more. I'd love
to hear your feedback on the book.
If you could leave it a quick review
on Amazon where I do read each and
every single review because this
helps me when creating more content
AND it also helps potential readers
make a decision when deciding if
this book will be a good fit for
them. This would mean a lot to me
and many other shoppers like
yourself!

Lastly, if you feel called to
explore protection and reversal
magick (which I highly recommend)
for your ongoing journey into
witchcraft and the realm of magick
then I suggest you grab my other
book called "Prayers and Protection
Magick to Destroy Witchcraft:
Banish Curses, Negative Energy &
Psychic Attacks; Break Spells, Evil
Soul Ties & Covenants; Protect &
Release Favors" You can find with

the   following   link:
https://www.amazon.com/dp/B096TRVG
GR

I wish you the best, my fellow
witch!

Cheers!
~Glinda Porter

RESOURCES

Cunningham, J. *Witchcraft For Beginners: A Basic Guide For Modern Witches For Find Their Own Path and Start Practicing To Learn Spells And Magic Rituals Using Esoteric And Occult Elements Like Herbs And Crystals.* 2019

Nietzsche, F. *Beyond Good and Evil: Prelude to a Philosophy of the Future*. 1886. Chapter IV. Apophthegms and Interludes. Section 146

Lipp, D. *The Complete Book of Spells: Wiccan Spells For Healing, Protection, and Celebration.* Rockridge Press 2020

Phillips, G. Open Your Eyes-All 3 Of Them.
Retrieved from
https://musingsfromtheuniverse.com/2021/03/08/open-your-eyes-all-3-of-them

Phillips, G. Something Wiccan This Way Comes-Part 1 of 2. Retrieved from https://musingsfromtheuniverse.com/2021/04/09/something-wiccan-this-way-comes-part-1-of-2

Shakespeare, W., & Gibson, R. (2005). Macbeth. Cambridge, UK: Cambridge University Press

Vanderbeck, P. *Green Witchcraft: A Practical Guide to Discovering the Magic of Plants, Herbs, Crystals, and Beyond.* Rockridge Press 2020

Whitehorn, M.L. Why Earth Is Closes To Sun in Dead of Winter. Retrieved from https://space.com

Wigington, P. (2020, August 26). 7 Ways To Develop Your Psychic Abilities. Retrieved from https://www.learnreligions.com/ways-to-develop-your-psychic-abilities-2561759

Wigington, P. (2020, August 28). Methods of Divination. Retrieved from https://www.learnreligions.com/methods-of-divination-2561764